THI
ISLAND LIFE

THIS

ISLAND LIFE

DISCOVERING BRITAIN'S OFFSHORE GEMS

Skokholm, Pembrokeshire • Cape Clear, Co. Cork • The Skelligs, Co. Kerry •
Garinish Island, Co. Cork • The Aran Islands, Co. Clare • Inishbofin and
Achill Island, Connemara • The Isle of Man • Walney Island, Cumbria

Written and illustrated by

MARY E. GILLHAM

HALSGROVE

First published in Great Britain in 2007
Copyright © 2007 Dr Mary E. Gillham

*Front cover: Main pictures shows Cape Clear Island
with the view to O'Driscoll's Castle.
Inset l-r: Basket making, Aran; Earl Purple
Orchid, Aran; Puffins, Skokholm; Donkey, Cape Clear.
Back cover: shows Dry stone walls on Inishmore*

British Library Cataloguing-in-Publication Data
A CIP record for this title is available from the British Library

ISBN 978 1 84114 619 5

HALSGROVE
Halsgrove House
Ryelands Industrial Estate
Bagley Road, Wellington, Somerset TA21 9PZ
Tel: 01823 653777   Fax: 01823 216796
email: sales@halsgrove.com
website: www.halsgrove.com

Printed and bound by
The Cromwell Press Ltd, Wiltshire

Contents

Introduction

This account addresses the natural history of a selection of islands along our Atlantic seaboard. These differ more fundamentally from each other than those considered in "Memories of Welsh Islands", Dinefwr 2005, which were primarily nature reserves, with seabirds, seals and flowery wildscapes having priority over human residents.

We start with another look at the princess of Welsh Islands, Skokholm off South Pembrokeshire. Visited again after a gap of nearly twenty years, we perceive changes in the grazing regime, the plant cover and especially the degree of comfort afforded to visiting naturalists. 2005 and 2006 were momentous years, when this island was purchased by the South and West Wales Wildlife Trust, which had been managing the bird observatory and nature reserve under various names as lessees for nearly half a century.

Most of the other islands are scattered along the scenic west coast of Ireland before we dip back into the Irish Sea and then north to the coast of Cumbria. By no means all are nature reserves although they include bird observatories and a botanists' paradise on Inisheer and Inishmor, nor do they all conform to the traditional idea of wild Ireland as peaty bog and acid moor.

Some do, like Inishbofin, lying off the mountain landscape of Connemara, where flocks of geese wing in from the North to graze the plantain swards in winter. So, too, is much of Cape Clear Island, the most southerly inhabited part of Ireland now that the Fastnet Lighthouse offshore has been automated. From the bird observatory there has come a valuable archive of the movements of birds of passage along its bleak but beautiful shores.

In sharp contrast is the natural rock garden and tiny walled fields of the Aran Islands, outliers of the world famous limestone pavement of the Burren in County Clare. Orchid, gentian, saxifrage, roseroot - need one say more?

Two islands close in space but worlds apart in landscape quality, are the Skelligs and Garinish Island. The precipitous bastions of the first rise like volcanoes from the turbulent ocean, one crowded with a multitude of noisy gannets, the other with the peaceful contemplation of sturdy beehive huts, built laboriously, stone on stone, by monks of old and with puffins meandering over campion covered slopes below.

Garinish, the island of hollies, lies in the beautiful enclave of Glengariff Bay, a dissected sea lough where seals lounge on shrub crowned islets. It has been developed as a fine Italian garden, blossoming in the embrace of the warm Atlantic Drift, which keeps frosts at bay.

Manx, isolated in the northern half of the Irish Sea, is a rather special but representative plot of typical, well loved British countryside. Its hedgerows burgeon with a wealth of hawthorn blossom in spring and wooded glens are insinuated into rich farmland. The bleaker hills bear crops of bilberries and there are cliffs and coves, sandy beaches and sea fishing to delight all visitors.

Walney Island, nudging the corner of the great sandy sweep of Morecambe Bay, is different again. Essentially a long sandspit, bordered by pebbles or saltmarsh, depending on the tidal wash, it is at the mercy of shifting sands rather than the spray sheeting up the rock faces of the others.

All have their own particular brand of wildscape elucidated in these pages. No one who has had the good fortune to see even some of them could fail to perceive the beauty and variety of these sea-girt outliers in comparison with the bright lights of the increasingly artificial modern world.

Dr Mary E. Gillham
Cardiff
2007

1
Skokholm Pembrokeshire
AN ISLAND REVISITED

It was early May in 2005 when an opportunity to return to Skokholm Island off South-west Wales materialised. That was where my addiction to islands had been born and had become firmly entrenched. It was my student stamping ground when I emerged from the forces and started training as an ecologist in the University of Wales.

I had first stepped ashore there almost sixty years before. By 1947 I had launched into a series of summers trying to assess how the crowded seabirds and vast rabbit population interacted with a vegetation suppressed by fierce salty gales.

Although visiting with parties of naturalists during the 1960s, 70s and 80s, it was probably twenty years since I had last set foot on that hallowed plot. It was time to catch up with the changes, as the menage of the field centre was updated to suit the more fastidious tastes of the modern age.

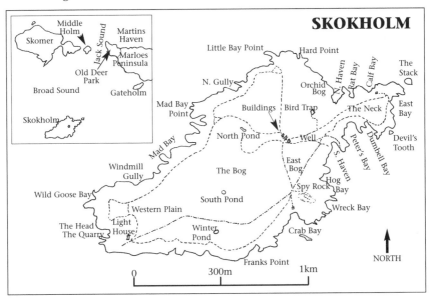

In times past the policy was not to make the living conditions too comfortable, or we should attract the wrong sort of people, but that was before the birth of the "Nanny State". Notwithstanding this, creature comforts do not come amiss with advancing years. The opportunity to 'test the waters' once more was too good to miss.

There was another of like mind whom I happened upon by chance as my plans were formulating. This was Jeffery Boswall, an early presenter of documentary series in the BBC Natural History Unit, a former head of the Film and Video Unit of the RSPB, doyen of bird song and leader of eco-tourism parties to some of the world's wildest places.

He had served as vice warden at the Skokholm Bird Observatory during a season in the early 1950s, helping Peter Conder, the warden, who later became head of the RSPB, with his wheatear research. Remembering me from those days, he asked a mutual acquaintance to reintroduce us.

No bells of recognition rang in the annals of my mind when we met. Faces have a way of changing over fifty years and people's names elude me still, as plant names, strangely, do not. Usually in the island community only christian names were divulged and the weeks were full of the comings and goings of desirable young men.

Those who regard islands as places to get away from people can be greatly mistaken. Not only may there be a constant stream of people, but of people of like mind. All are drawn by the same lure, the concept of a natural community of birds and mammals developing in its own fashion, far from the interfering humans who fill the mainland with their machines and effluents. Half a century had produced no fundamental changes in our outlook and Jeffery and I resolved to join up. The date of our visit was fixed by the availability of accommodation.

On the day that our early afternoon boat sailed, he, as the current chairman of the Avon County Wildlife Trust, was scheduled to lead a dawn chorus walk. This was in Towerhouse Wood, Somerset, at 4.0 am, promoted by the Woodland Trust in aid of charity. A cryptic note written in small type on the poster advertising the event read: "The party will disband at 06.30 hours when the leader will be going home to bed."

In fact the leader got himself to Nailsea and Bristol and caught a train to Cardiff, where I met him on the platform for the 08.45 train to the West. This was Saturday, a day on which "work on the line" was likely to disrupt travel. It did. We would have to de-train at Carmarthen and proceed by bus to pick up another at Neyland for Haverfordwest at the end of the line.

Fortunately the modern wonder of the mobile phone enabled us to alert the South and West Wales Wildlife Trust, who are responsible for running the observatory and we were met in Carmarthen, to ensure that we made it to the boat on time.

Sugarback, the lighthouse pony, who once upon a time had hauled the luggage trolley up from the landing place, had long since passed from this world to a pony paradise. He had been replaced by a sequence of mechanical 'dumpers', the latest of which was suffering from a temporarily defunct engine.

Thus it was that we found ourselves in a Haverfordwest Garden Centre acquiring wheelbarrows, to be manhandled up to the living quarters in lieu. After prolonged wrangling, we emerged with one new and one secondhand and managed somehow to get them stowed into the back of the van beside a motley of stores topped by our travel bags.

Miraculously, we arrived at Martinshaven well ahead of schedule and settled by the stone gatepost leading into the Old Deer park to eat our sandwiches.

No longer was the transit boat small enough to pull into the beach. It had been replaced by the "Dale Princess", a fifty seater MCA licenced passenger vessel. The fifty seats accommodated fifty bodies for several journeys in quick succession on day trips to Skomer Island. I was on one such myself a few weeks later, when many would-be passengers were left behind to await the next boat. For Skokholm, however, we were fewer, with fifteen the maximum number of visitors, and much of the accommodation was occupied by stores or a few folk who came 'just for the ride'.

An iron gangway had been constructed over deeper water off the adjacent headland, this reached by a narrow stepped path along the intervening stretch of cliff. The sea was like the proverbial millpond, the only choppiness occurring as we rounded the point of the Old Deer Park into the notoriously restless waters of Jack Sound.

No longer were there friendly lighthousekeepers on South Haven quay to help with the luggage. Those worthies had been made redundant, as on all lighthouses with the coming of automation. A bunch of stalwarts transferred the ingoing gear onto the shore, to be handed up along a chain of a dozen or so visitors returning to the mainland. The outgoing packages, set well aside to avoid a mix-up, were lowered aboard, and we newcomers allowed ashore. Seldom had I experienced such a placid sea at this juncture.

I missed the announcement of a general briefing session when everything had been trundled up to the Wheelhouse in the newly acquired barrows or on willing shoulders. Instead, I was marvelling at the fundamental change of plant life around the old lime kiln.

1. *Wild Golden Rod*

Fresh shoots of golden rod, formerly rare on the island, covered almost the whole of this slope. I had expected minor changes, but nothing on this scale. Four months later, I learned that almost the entire island was gilded by the yellow flower spikes of this composite in August and September.

All the larger livestock had been removed, the big Soay sheep flock, the smaller goat herd, the cow and the pony. Rabbits were still as prolific as ever. Could the absence of their larger companions be responsible for so fundamental a difference?

Wandering off, bemused by the change, I missed out on the tea and cakes that accompanied the imparting of information. When I was perceived missing the young wardens were picturing an absent-minded octogenarian following tracks used in the past but unsuited to less nimble feet. They need not have worried. I was enjoying a gentle potter, lost in a nostalgic world of half a century before.

I was rudely awakened from my reverie as I negotiated an unexpected spread of bog in the vicinity of East Pond. Pacing determinedly towards me, long neck outstretched and honking belligerently, was a male Canada goose - jealously guarding his home plot. Behind him his mate sat on a nest of eggs among rushy tussocks.

These are Britain's largest geese. No way was I to be allowed anywhere near, the angry shaking of wing feathers and lowering of the head pressed the point.

2. *Belligerant Canada Geese*

The influx of *Branta canadensis* across the mainland in the last few decades has been phenomenal, but the birds were reputed to move to the coast, if at all, only in winter and not to nest. These were setting a precedent. Chasing them off would have proved ineffective with those great wings to bring them back to their chosen holiday home away from the common rabble.

I learned later that the strategy adopted here was for a brave soul to breach the proud father's defences, take the big white eggs and hard boil them. They were then replaced in the nest, to all appearances unchanged. This kept the couple earnestly protecting them, the goose doing all the incubation and the gander guarding her for the four weeks or so until hatching. He should continue in this role when she leads the string of goslings away.

How much longer than the requisite four weeks would it take this pair to realise that they had no prospect of doing this and providing potential recruits for a future Skokholm colony? (The brood, although usually five or six, can number up to eleven.) My "Handbook of British Birds", published in the 1940s, states Canada geese to be rare in Wales. This no longer applies, some of the winter flocks flying over the Cardiff Reservoirs now being impressively large.

Merely confiscating the eggs might have tempted them to lay more , although they are normally single brooded. As eight nesting pairs were already scattered around the island, this could have been the start of big trouble.

Keeping a respectful distance, I headed on to Crab Bay and descended to the little bird hide perched at the edge of the dipping cliff. This is a primary puffin viewing site, but 7th May was early yet and the three hundred or so birds present were loafing on the placid water just offshore. Every now and again one popped from a nearby burrow and shot off to sea. There was no hanging about: none of the qizzical head turning to see what was going on all around, as later in the season.

In a week or so the slope would be crowded with plump interactive bodies. There was safety in numbers, but birds bold enough to investigate the potential of setting up home on today's blatanty empty slope were understandably nervous. They were built for a life at sea; this nesting lark was an unwelcome chore. Who knows? A family of rabbits might have taken up residence in last year's hole while they were wintering out at sea? Some flew in and popped down a hole as I watched, but lingered only momentarily before scuttling out to seek haven among their waterborne fellows.

I wandered back to the path, taking the fork on the other side of East Pond, where I was still regarded suspiciously by the pugnacious gander. The site itself was different. Hitherto East Pond had been clearly demarcated, a small body of open water, with the island's only colony of royal fern tucked in under the vertical bank.

Now the sides had collapsed and the water seeped out all ways, transforming the former grass:heather moor into a spreading quagmire - this even muddying a dip in the main path to the farmhouse.

Could the geese be responsible? Had those big webbed feet trampled the banks, plugged the outlet stream and puddled the trapped water into a squishy sward of marsh pennywort and other water plants? How long, I wondered, had they been in residence here? When I later caught up with the modern map of the island I saw that the very name had been altered from East Pond to East Bog.

This was part of the changing face of the island. The short grass of Crab Bay, speckled with sea campion and sea pansies and shortly to live up to its other name of Puffin Town as the feathered mob assembled onshore, was a reassuring part of the island I had known when I first fell under its spell

The Farmhouse common room was as welcoming as ever - or moreso with its draped curtains and well plumped-up cushions. I ascended half the steps leading to the Angel Loft, part ladder and part stairway, only to be brought up short by the debris above. Traditionally the women's sleeping quarters, the upper floor was now out of bounds - structurally unsound, so they said.

I had been allocated a double bedded room opposite the main entrance all to myself. In it were two armchairs (luxury), two floor mats and the familiar rough timber washstand with basin and jug and vessel for getting water from the sealed rain tank outside, not withstanding that this was hermetically sealed by the rusting up of the tap, so that water had to be brought from the Wheelhouse.

Jeffery, nostalgic for the tiny rabbit hutch of a room where he had been domiciled during his months as a teen age assistant, swapped with Ted , a retired vicar with strong botanical leanings, who was rewarded with a room almost as palatial as mine. As the former's stated intention was to catch up on lost sleep during the first few days, he was happy enough. There was space to do little else within those four close-set walls, where there was no room to swing a cat and no cat to swing now that the lighthousekeepers' black moggy had passed away. I know, because those had sometimes been my quarters in the past.

More buildings had arisen to accommodate the larger clientele, which included the fifteen visitors and three volunteer helpers as well as Jo, the warden, and David, her partner, who was officially public relations officer and cook-caterer.

The wheel of the "Alice Williams", the famous pre-war wreck, still adorned the Wheelhouse wall over the spacious fireplace, now presiding over two monster deep freezers. Alice herself, the carved figurehead from the ship's bow, had lost her pristine freshness as a sea mark on the whitewashed rock face in Hog Bay and had been refurbished to adorn the high wall at the opposite end, in a well earned retirement out of the wind and the rain.

The Baron's Workshop, old time glory hole for the very necessary tools, timber and equipment, had been connected by a new doorway at the end of the long, well scrubbed dining table. That space was now the kitchen-cum-pantry, with a large double sink, where we took turns washing up. 'Spud bashing' was no longer one of the chores undertaken by visitors.

The Bunkhouse, traditionally the men's dormitory, was now the warden's quarters. A line of single and double rooms had been built against the yard wall, one with work benches instead of beds and designated as the Lab, although offering little more than working space. A structure against another wall housed the paraphernalia from the Baron's Workshop, the Baron being one of the unforgettable characters from Ronald Lockley's pre-war sojourn on the island.

After his day the observatory went into abeyance during the war. When it reopened in the immediate post war years, those of us converging on it were of a generation returning from an adventurous past, in or out of the armed forces, or living away from home with an evacuated school. We were used to fending for ourselves and making the most of facilities now regarded as inadequate

It had been no problem for us to walk down to the pool of sparkling water that served as the well and carry slopping buckets up to the buildings. Although shared with a few thirsty herbivores and birds, the spring water had been pronounced free from harmful organisms and we thrived on it. This water, that bubbled from the bowells of the earth half way between the buildings and the landing, seeped through the under-sea rock strata from the mainland - as proved by red eosin dye introduced at source.

Matters are very different in this meticulously hygienic age, when folk are presumed to lack the armoury of protective antibodies with which previous generations were well endowed. The well is now lidded, the water pumped up the slope to a storage tank inside instead of outside the yard. The larger modern tank is furnished with a tap - no climbing up to dip buckets into the top - and is delivered into the Wheelhouse through more pipes and taps.

Even this is deemed insufficient precaution. All drinking water is now boiled, cooled and decanted into sealed flagons, from which we could help ourselves, using glass tumblers instead of enamel mugs.

Maybe it is even filtered en route, to sift out another, quite benign, new arrival which thrives where the water spills out from underground. This is an American alien, the least duckweed *(Lemna minuta)*, whose tiny green fronds are less than half the size of those of the native lesser duckweed *(Lemna minor)*, with which they mingle.

Both would be beavering away in an aerating capacity, a benefit formerly performed by the frogspawn algae *(Batrachospermum monili-forme)*, one of the few red algae which lives in fresh water, but usually only where this bubbles, unsullied, from an underground spring.

For the squeamish with no faith in the old regime, there is nothing to worry about any longer. Jo Havard and David Milborough, who ran the establishment like clockwork in 2005, were both trained in modern hygiene and culinary practice. No longer did we gather watercress from the streams. Green salad arrived in packs, despatched from a supermarket under sheets of cling film - a practice seldom indulged in by normal thrifty housewives who prefer their 'greens' unprocessed.

No longer did rabbit pie, gulls' eggs and goat's milk figure on the menu as in those pioneering days. The back-up staff ordering the stores onshore had rendered these self supporting activities that we so relished redundant. Today's bread came ready sliced and wrapped, offering no chance to any successor of Caroline, the Welsh Black cow, to sneak the first few mouthfuls on the quay. No-one was complaining. The cuisine was excellent, the menus varied and the repasts skilfully prepared.

Duvets had replaced the need for visitors to bring down sleeping bags, though we still supplied our own bed linen and towels - understandably, with the much doctored water supply no more plentiful than before. A calor gas fired boiler simmered in a corner of the Wheelhouse at certain times, supplying hot water for personal hygiene.

There was calor gas lighting instead of portable tilly lamps in the public rooms, but the two wall lamps in my bedroom lacked enough pressure to stay alight for more than a few minutes. I was glad of the trusty torch, the candle wedged in a small bottle and box of matches that I had brought to tide me over such little problems.

I was awakened at the same time each morning by a very forthcoming wren. Full of the joys of spring, he came with his wake-up song to the window sill within a few feet of my pillow, this an extension of his home range in the farmhouse garden to leeward. In fact I woke with the dawn at 5.0 am, although my windows faced west and onto the shaded knoll that rose sharply to the south. What better opportunity for observing wildlife in comfort?

3. *Preening rabbits*

The Knoll was hopping with rabbits and nowhere could I have enjoyed more intimate viewing. Some looked me straight in the eye through the glass. Others went through a complicated preening ritual, contorting their bodies into unnatural poses to reach every part that might have been sullied by the noisy, messy gulls that were their constant companions.

All jumped over the nettle patches rather than pushing through, often taking off from a standing start in a high, graceful arc. It must have been their pink noses that were sensitive, because the nettles' slender poison-filled hairs could not have penetrated their fur. Baby rabbits have to learn not to eat nettles and could be watched experimenting with them and recoiling as they triggered the turgid hairs to expel their toxin.

Everything was mating, though the rabbits didn't have to wait until the spring for that. One little fellow sat patiently beside his chosen partner as she nibbled the already overgrazed turf. She remained quiescent when he mounted but, after a successful bout of thrusting, he lost his balance and slid off backwards, his little white scut flattened under his rounded rump. The same happened the next time round and he threw two little white paws in the air in frustration as he toppled off once again.

4. *Whoops!*

Having got my eye in, I realised that this sort of thing was going on all the time. The rabbits were so thick on the ground in many parts, that we just didn't bother to watch them any longer.

A pair of pied wagtails attracted to the lawn-like sward outside the window seemed to be similarly employed. The paler one was passive, the other taking short zig-zag runs at her, with wings spread sideways, then fluttering with tail fanned as he pressed his breast to the ground and extended his beak towards her. There was no mounting, so this may have been some one-sided aggression. As they took off the little birds were tossed about by the brisk breeze and blown back onto the sloping Knoll.

Many of the herring and lesser black-backed gulls were certainly mating. Hen birds seemed willing on the whole, allowing their mate to place his big webbed feet somewhat precariously on her back, his wings flapping violently as he tried to maintain balance.

Sometimes the two stood side by side, nibbling each others bills, faced each other for a head bobbing session or moved slowly forwards stroking each others necks with their beaks. Gulls mate for life and such intimacies serve to strengthen the pair bond.

Warden Jo led the party on an exploratory walk around the island on the first morning, but the other ritual weekly outings of crossing by plank to the Stack and 'shearwatering' at night no longer figured. In the past boats usually came only on Saturdays, bringing visitors for a full week. Most now came for three nights or four, so these routine jaunts would have to be doubled up, leaving staff with little time to get on with necessary maintenance work, so had been discontinued.

Old time wardens and cooks were on permanent duty until they went ashore at the end of the season. Modern ones had two day spells with no visitors, to give them a break or time to catch up with chores. Whitewashing the buildings facing onto the Wheelhouse yard was in progress during our four night stay.

The guided walk was no longer a tour of the high spots. We scrunched noisily along the main road to the lighthouse as far as this went, then cut across the west end and Western Plain, well inland and back through the island centre, missing out on the spectacular Mad Bay cliffs and flowers, Littlebay Point, Orchid Bog, the Neck and other special features.

It seemed very humdrum compared with the Peter Conder style introductory walks, sniffing along walls for storm petrels, climbing down to herring gull nests, leaning over brinks to look at guillemot ledges and the like. Happening twice as often, the thrill of introducing the little highlights is bound to pale. Nest sites of a pair of buzzards and a pair of peregrines were indicated, but we did not see the birds, nor the merlin and sparrow hawk that have been reported.

The ravens on the west end were more accommodating and we were able to watch the three chicks riding the wind on their early flights. A few raptors and Corvids have been here over the years but the choughs were new. It was good to see them in the same area as the ravens, giving us the opportunity to compare size and grace of movements. These elegant birds with their crimson appendages are spreading around the South

5. Choughs

Wales coast very satisfactorily at present, south into Glamorgan and north to Ceredigion (the old Cardiganshire).

A brace of shelduck flew over as we skirted Crab Bay, a pair of these thought to be nesting thereabouts. As dabblers on mudflats, we are used to seeing these nesting in rabbit burrows on Flatholm Island off Cardiff, well up the Severn Estuary, but they were newcomers here, welcome both as natives and as ornamentals, with their black, white and chestnut plumage.

Other new residents were the two wood pigeons nesting in a cave and scarcely to be expected on a virtually treeless island. They did not show themselves this morning. Jackdaws and starlings had been always with us, but the blackbirds were something of a novelty.

After Sunday lunch Jeffery retired to his cubby hole to continue sleeping off his work load. Anticipating a respite from battling with the wind, I took myself to Spy Rock, which rises high enough out of the plateau to afford shelter from whatever wind should blow. I lingered first behind a rock outlier savouring the splendid panorama back across Broad Sound.

From this angle of viewing the distinct outline of St. David's Head loomed in the gap between Skomer and Middleholm with the sun-kissed Deer Park further away to the right across Jack Sound. The primal rock face towering over me was shaggy from top to toe with upstanding lichens. Sea campion softened the leeward faces, which came hummocking down to the great drift of bluebells at its foot.

I climbed the steep little path to the summit, from where expansive views encompassed 360 degrees, including a great vault of china blue sky. The Pembrokeshire coast stretched away south past Gateholm and St. Ann's Head and across the mouth of Milford Haven. Legs braced against the wind, I still nearly got blown away, despite the gentleness of the waves murmuring among the rocks below, so I did not linger.

Along the little trodden path to Wreck Bay I moved slowly, to avoid putting up the gulls from among the bluebells. They were in the early stages of nesting as yet, with no hatchlings to feed, and were standing around in couples, savouring the peace before serious foraging and defence of the growing family began. Only the piercing call of an oyster catcher drifting up from the shore broke the stillness of the afternoon.

Later, as I settled into a comfortable nook where I could lean back against a smooth boulder, a clamorous mob of gulls gathered at a little distance from the shore. Birds were dropping from the air into a flurry of surface-shoaling fish. Razorbills had been there before them, dipping down to cash in on the food bonanza without having to dive for it. Then a shag came skimming across the water to join in the fun.

The little silvered turrets of foam disappeared as the fish shoal withdrew to safer depths, with some of the razorbills plunging down after it. One of them set about a thorough preening. Rolling over onto each side in turn, it splashed water over its head, back and tail, like a blackbird in a woodland puddle. Being afloat, it could afford a good rinse, which it achieved by rolling over onto its back to show only the white belly, its head and tail submerged and the webbed feet paddling uselessly in the air above. Spending so much time in the water, it should not have needed to indulge in such ablutions until the chalky excrement began to build up in the nesting crevices.

This activity ceased when a boatload of tourists approached for a closer view of the puffins, always everybody's favourites. I lay back among the bluebells, watching the chittering swallows looming across the heavens. The two shelducks circled Spy Rock several times. This was obviously their chosen patch. As burrow nesters, they might give a homecoming puffin a nasty shock on its first exploratory visit to the old nest hole.

Bumble bees were busy working the sea campion flowers, but I saw no butterflies, even here, out of the wind. Gangly black St. Marks flies were about, these recognisable by the long black legs trailing out behind.

A few crop pellets were strewn along the edge of the lesser black-back colony. The largest was of fish bones and otoliths* and must have been coughed up by the greater black-back that lorded it over this, the island's highest knob. Smaller ones were of chaff and plant remains, speckled with beetle elytra.

Many of the gulls were flying in with nesting material and I came across a broken egg, probably purloined from a neighbour's nest. Only one bird was sufficiently belligerent to fly out to the attack, screaming like a Viking raider each time I followed the path between gullery and

*Otoliths are white, calcareous objects the size and shape of large wheat grains, formed in the inner ear of fish taken as prey. (And also in the statocysts of various invertebrates.)

goose nest. Had he taken his cue from the gander? Apparently he had developed this habit with all who passed and had been christened "Bonkers" by the resident staff. Perhaps his domestic menage was a little ahead of the other's and the general pandemonium would begin in earnest as more eggs hatched.

6. *Lesser black-backed gull*

The sun shone brilliantly throughout our stay but the wind remained unrelenting. When in long term residence I had become acclimatised to this and thought nothing of it when others were suffering. Now I had lost my immunity and was one of the sufferers. The handiest place for shedding a few layers and enjoying the sunshine was on the bench outside the Wheelhouse, with a mug of tea in one hand and a slice of home made cake in the other. But that was a mid-afternoon treat.

Jeffery and I set off round the island at a liesurely pace after breakfast on Monday. I had descended obliquely to the Crab Bay hide on Saturday. This time we went the orthodox way, alongside the rope pegged to the ground, to give the unsteady a helping hand on the steeper bits in wet weather. At the top we found a wooden block pierced by three holes with three matching pegs alongside. Following the instructions, we put two pegs in two holes, indicating to passers by that two persons were in the hide below, preferably not to be disturbed.

A short spell there and we proceeded west, where the abundance of young sorrel plants suggested that the central plateau might turn a rusty red later in the season, as it had in 1950 and 1979 - if not swamped by the invading golden rod. Swallow flocks were hawking flies over Winter Pond, so called because it dried out in summer, and more Canada geese came flapping across.

Perched on a rock beyond the lighthouse, catching up on the past sixty years, we spotted the first swift of the summer. These aerial miracles had no doubt been passing through during every one of those sixty years, and had just as surely been dutifully recorded in the island log. It put us in our place as transient interlopers into a tried and trusted system of ongoing life.

The choughs and ravens put on a fine show of aerobatics and there were more Canada geese nesting in thicker cover by North Pond, the

7. *Skylarks*

ganders less inclined to take offence than the first of my acquaintance. Wheatears, the subject of my companion's earlier studies here, were still hopping jauntily around the short grass swards and herringbone walls, no doubt doing all the things that he had recorded in his field notebook so long ago.

Meadow pipits and rock pipits were about, drab as ever, but always busy.

Skylarks were in good voice, emitting short warbles as they ascended and pouring out their full song as they swooped earthwards. There were none of the prolonged utterances as they hung motionless on fluttering wings overhead - the music of the spheres which is the epitome of pastoral summer scenes.

We put this down to the gale. To remain motionless at that height in that wind would need more than a fluttering of those diminutive wings. They would have to be flying actively upwind at the same speed that the airstream was blowing them back, in order to hold their position. Such prolonged carolling must need more energy than could be spared if they were so engaged.

Sadly, practically all the heather had disappeared from the east and centre of the island. One of my anti-grazing exclosures erected in the 1950s had been sited on a considerable sized plot of heather. The bushes inside remained intact while those inhibited by grazing outside became overhwelmed by bracken. Now the whole community had been grazed to extinction. Was this why the Soay sheep had been removed, and if so, when?

Certainly there was no sign of the regeneration of young plants, as there surely would be by May if there were any left to sprout. On Skomer a few weeks later, I noticed the same phenomenon. A large enclosure there, fenced against rabbits, protected a healthy stand of heather, but little or none remained outside.

Some plants are hardier and there were plenty of flowers on the red campion and ground ivy, as well as the bluebells. A few lesser celandines, heath violets and early forget-me-nots were a tail over from April. Thrift was not yet at prime except on inaccessible cliff faces, where flowers were in no danger of being nibbled off. Sea mayweed and rock spurrey showed a little colour and large areas simulating bare soil supported those two species that are most resistant to the pressures which induced this - the sea storksbill and buck's horn plantain.

After lunch I headed for one of the few parts of the island offering a simulation of scrubland suitable for small woodland birds. This was the now overgrown Heligoland bird trap on the approach to the Neck. Rabbits could still enter the broad end of the roofed wire netting funnel, but it was wet underfoot there and not many were tempted.

In the absence of larger herbivores which are not averse to getting their feet wet, vegetation had burgeoned, this including a few woody species. Yellow flags were just coming into bloom. These had formerly provided the main cover on the marsh, as bracken did on the rest.

As conditions improved for trapping and ringing passerines, however, birds were no longer trapped, this by request of the island's owner. Hemlock water dropwort had increased apace alongside the Irises. This species is poisonous to most grazers, but little had ventured outside the partial protection of the netting. The sallow bushes were rather sorry looking specimens, but a sycamore was struggling up among the nettles. The rounded red bud scales not yet pushed off by the expanding leaves resembled berries from a distance.

A whitethroat had taken up temporary residence and ignored my approach, the rather scratchy little song continuing unabated. It occurred to me that this was because there was nowhere else to go that offered suitable whitethroat habitat, apart from the scrubby growths around the buildings. I had seen it there too. It may have come to regard the human presence as a necessary corollary to useful vegetation in which to skulk.

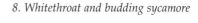

8. Whitethroat and budding sycamore

Another which commuted across the stretch of the Home Meadow between these two leafy sanctuaries was a willow warbler, which sometimes appeared outside my window in the early morning. In the trap this favoured the denser cover of a flowering gorse bush rising from drier ground, where old Bovista puffballs, still containing a good content of spores, were being bowled around by the wind.

Vegetation beside the stream draining the newly burgeoning thicket was much as before. Water forget-me-not and lesser spearwort pushed through the raft of bronzed pondweed leaves, while water starwort stems wove among the green tiddliwinks of marsh pennywort leaves.

After the evening meal we gathered in the common room trying to make up our minds whether to go 'shearwatering' or not. We had chickened out the previous night after sampling the wind. The shearwaters' breeding calender is ahead of the puffins' and the birds were already sitting on eggs. Forty five thousand pairs was the number estimated to be nesting on Skokholm at this time, and a hundred thousand pairs on Skomer.

It was the night of the new moon and the sky was as cloudless as it had been all day, though the nagging wind had not abated. As darkness fell, the planets, stars and finally the milky way materialised, with the lighthouse beams slicing through the void below.

This was the sort of sky one admires in the Tropics, far from the street lights of home, but temperature destroyed the illusion today. Tony Povey, lecturer in business studies from Ascot, but formerly living in Cardiff, commented on how little of this celestial panorama we could see through the nocturnal orange haze that now enshrouded the capital of the Principality.

I recalled the words of a certain cleric lamenting the absence of the skyscapes that he had enjoyed as a boy. His prayer to the Almighty began:"Darken our lightness we beseech thee oh Lord".

We searched our memories for such astronomy as we had learned in the scouts or guides, when some of the more shapely constellations could be easily recognised - though sometimes, even then, more likely from our summer camps than our urban residences. It was not the great swathes of orange street lamps that masked them then, but industrial smog and the fumes from myriad coal fires burning on domestic hearths.

Several shearwaters plumped to earth around us as we stood by the Knoll. This discrete colony had been closely studied over the years, starting with Lockley himself. Staggering results had accrued from birds being taken half way round the world in aircraft, finding their way home over unknown territory under their own steam, to be found back in their burrows in a couple of days.

9. Manx Shearwater

Seven of us, not including Jeffery, who was asleep by then, elected to go shearwater watching. This involved a tramp to the other end of the island where the birds were thickest on the ground and where the soft red of the landwardly directed lighthouse beams indicated when we were getting too near the cliff edge.

On such occasions there were no complaints about that much overworked old 'tramroad' across the island. Armed though we were with powerful torches, it would have been easy to come a cropper in one of the many burrows if trying to follow lesser paths. Most of the torches were masked with transparent red films when we went into action. This was a new innovation since the days when we needed to temporarily dazzle the birds in order to pick them up for ringing. Now we only needed to observe them from a few feet away.

This was not only because the owner was against bird ringing. So many hundreds, probably thousands, of these ocean wanderers had been ringed in past decades, many of them re caught as recoveries, that it was deemed unnecessary to continue. Much had already been learned of their life histories, migration routes and longevity. One from a Welsh island was found to have clocked up fifty three, while some related 'tube-nosed' fulmars were known to exceed fifty years. Such long lives in birds little bigger than pigeons is remarkable, although they would need to live a lot longer to out-compete some of the world's not much larger parrots.

On so dark a night, when there was no clamour from wakeful predatory gulls, I felt there should have been more shearwaters about than there were. On nights of full moon and no cloud cover, many gulls stay awake and few of the 'tubenoses' were likely to risk coming ashore. Those that did might well join the many carcases littered round the ponds where the gulls took them to be consumed.

I was surprised how many fewer there were than I remembered. This may have been because the birds were still incubating and did not need to be relieved as frequently as when there was a young chick to be fed. That period lasted longer and much of the past ringing had been carried out when the young were leaving the burrows. Ringing these instead of adults had the advantage that their age would be known when they were recaught. The brooding adult and chick might wait for as much as five nights before the partner returned with food.

A thriving colony of storm petrels nested in Quarry Bay below the lighthouse, but it was too hazardous to go down there in the dark and we were not lucky enough to see any flying past on the clifftop.

The others were not disappointed with the small number. I had set my sights too high, having been thoroughly spoiled among the New Zealand Maoris' sooty shearwaters and the Aboriginals' short tailed shearwaters on the islands between mainland Australia and Tasmania. (See "A Naturalist in New Zealand", 1966, Museum Press and "Island Hopping in Tasmania's Roaring Forties", 2000, Stockwell.)

With shelter at such a premium, larger plants tended to congregate in the old garden. Repeated attempts had been made to keep the rabbits out of this with deeply sunk wire netting both inside and outside the sturdy earth and stone walls, but these defences were soon breached by a highly competitive population spurred on by hunger. Some horticulturally inclined warden:cook teams had managed to raise a few vegetable crops over the years, but they fought a losing battle.

Currently the garden was untended and essentially derelict. One of the yawning holes excavated amidships by rabbits was covered over with a board to prevent people from falling in. I lifted this to peer inside and surprised two well grown slow worms snoozing beneath. These are common enough under discarded sheets of corrugated iron on Flatholm, but such debris is frowned upon on Skokholm and they were not easy to find here.

There had always been a stag-headed sycamore tucked against the northern wall and now there were several. The largest was smaller than I remembered, though somewhat gnarled for a newcomer. The usual robust growth rate of its compatriots on the mainland might work in reverse here as hopeful new shoots were cut back by the wind. The nest box in a low fork was swathed in lichens, but held no nest. Other woody species were a meagre sloe, a Hydrangea and a currant bush with a few green flowers.

Another lifted board revealed twenty-one *Helix aspersa* garden snails clamped to the underside, these capable of devouring a goodly amount of the fugitive herbage when they sallied forth at night. Grasses had been allowed to grow long, but the haulms had collapsed into a spongy mass, where a blackbird raised a mini dust storm as it scraped away for goodies beneath.

The little garden pool remained and its central island was the favourite perch of a willow warbler, with paler eye stripe and legs than the chiff chaff, which was also about. The stone where he lingered so frequently was surrounded by a bubbly froth of green algae. Tallest of the herbs were self sown rushes and yellow Irises.

Wheatears came to perch on the walls with their topknots of sea campion and more snails shared the crevices with upstanding spikes of wall pennywort, their spires of white bells like undersized Yuccas. Navel wort, an alternative name for this member of the stonecrop family arose from the fleshy circular leaves with central dimple.

Daffodils and Narcissus are distasteful to rabbits and had survived over the years.

Now some of their larger cousins were rampaging out of the garden and across the Home Paddock to the Wheelhouse yard. Flowers were finished by May, but were said to have consisted of long yellow coronas surrounded by six white petals. More imposing than average, their pedigree remained a mystery.

2005's most prolific plant life grew alongside the high stone walls linking the groups of buildings, and in the Wheelhouse yard. There was a very good reason for this. It was a product of the increasing human population served by but two Elsans - an updated model in stylish blue.

Alongside this was a drawing of a gentleman sitting on the loo reading a newspaper. The caption read: *"This toilet is meant to be sat on. Gentlemen wishing to stand, please water the nettles."* And how the nettles had revelled in these simple acts of generosity!

They were romping out from all connecting walls and had filled the Wheelhouse yard apart from the main throughway and two small tracks, one to a new hut where secondhand books were sold and one to an old hen house where poultry were no longer kept. No wonder those baby rabbits were having a hard time of it.

Elders were not far behind the all conquering nettles, these being characteristic "followers of man" and his livestock. Fuchsia, Buddleja, sallows and sycamores pushed up in their shelter, further boosted by the tipped bowls of washing water and the occasional apple peel that were helping to build up a rich compost.

A goldcrest was sometimes to be seen among the twigs outside the bookshop, while sedge warbler and wren had joined the chiff chaff and whitethroat in the taller shrubs. Someone reported a spotted flycatcher.

Former wardens had fenced off and cultivated a strip alongside the high wall where the old water tank had stood, but this had lapsed into disuse. Greater willow herb and even sweet cicely, usually found a great deal further north, were cashing in on the husbanded soil, but their days were numbered.

Irene Payne, a hardworking volunteer, resident in the Prescelly Hills, had embarked on a project to restore this garden's former glory. Whenever we passed she was busy inside the rabbit mesh fence digging. She rescued persistent chives, parsley and chards, digging round some and replanting others, but there was more.

Working as she chatted to those who encouraged from the sidelines, she exposed around ten newts, skulking under a board smaller than that appropriated by the garden slow worms. Human litter can be a boon to wildlife. Some were little more than efts, exhibiting no diagnostic features, but only palmate newts were known to occur on the island.

10. *Juvenile palmate newts and chickweed*

In the early morning chill a caterpillar covered with short grey bristles was spotted dangling upside down on a willow branch from the claspers of its ultimate body segment. As the day warmed up, it swung its head around and moved on up the branch, presumably to latch on somewhere cryptic to pupate. Perhaps the increasing chill of nightfall had put a stop to its upward progress the previous day. Most 'woolly bears' are encountered on the ground.

A likely guess was an oak eggar, which has no need of oak, despite its name. In southern England these caterpillars hatch from the eggs in August and go into hibernation when quite small, growing on during the following summer to pupate and produce moths in August. Here, however, in the west and north, where lower temperatures slow down metabolism, caterpillars over-winter the first year and pass the second winter as pupae, ready to mature in the following May or June.

It is probably the neat oval shape of the silken cocoon, like a large acorn, that is responsible for the appelation of 'oak'. This is spun among the twigs of the sallow on which the caterpillar feeds or on the ground, but the ground was not a very safe place here with all that digging going on. The staff resolved to keep an eye on it and see what sort of moth emerged.

The only shrubs escaping from the environs of the buildings and Heligoland trap were elders - shrubs which have made big advances in recent years on Flatholm, Steepholm and Puffin Island off Anglesey. Some on and around the Knoll were quite leafless on the windward side, but must have enjoyed a long enough spell of calm weather to grow in the first place - implying summer growth and winter kill.

Shoots arise in pairs so the outermost may shrivel while the inner ones grow, to help fill the core of a tightly wind-trimmed bush very different from the average hedgerow elderberry.

These caricatures of arboreal growths are landmarks in the rabbits' treeless world, as are rock outcrops and vegetated anthills, trysting sites or gathering grounds for the exchange of pheromones. In their shelter couples might chase round and round in ever diminishing circles, sometimes tripping over each other. It was temptingto think that one of the pair might be a doe playing 'hard to get'.

Next day I explored some less frequented parts of the north coast. The cliffs around North Haven held special memories. Springtime vegetation rises to a crescendo here in the deeply incised gullies and the stream spilling over from Orchid Bog, which had been known to entice elvers up from the sea into a dead end leading nowhere suitable for them to grow into adult eels.

Evidently orchids no longer grew here, although the name had not been changed on the current map. The 1950s had seen several hundred spikes of the massed, deep purple blossoms. They had been a favourite nosh for the juicy black slugs *(Arion ater)* that marched forth in their hordes during rain or as dew began to fall. Had these been responsible for the orchids' demise?

It seems likely that even then the sward that we so admired did not represent an original population. Experts had identified them as hybrids between the early marsh and the common spotted orchids *(Dactylorhiza incarnata X D. fuchsii)*. This implies the presence of the two parent species in earlier times. Neither are known to have been found here in the post war years, so this, in itself, suggests a change from a former state.

Vertical faces in North Bay, Rat Bay and Calf Bay are inaccessible to rabbits and this was very evident in the current exuberance of plant life. Mounds of thrift and sea campion were lush pincushions of uninhibited flowers, with no sign of the rampant newly arrived golden rod.

Here, sheltered also from most of the salty winds, were primroses at their prime, a living rock garden of spring yellow tucked among the purple-red outcrops of Devonian old red sandstone. Windmill Gully further west along this north coast was another renowned primrose site, reached by a secret path undulating over the base of various headlands. There was sufficient saltiness there to nourish sea milkwort *(Glaux maritima)* and brookweed *(Samolus valerandi)*, both in the Primulaceae but unusual bedfellows of the primroses of our unsalted woodland dells.

11. *Primroses*

A major new innovation west of North Haven was a flight of steps leading up from sea level to the bluebell sward with its myriad nesting gulls above. Boats had formerly come in to the narrow beach in North Haven when easterly weather put the quay in South Haven out of bounds.

A similar new entry had been constructed on Skomer Island - a flight of steps up the cliffs west of the old beach landing in that island's North Haven. Those I saw for the first time a few weeks later - jostling to ascend with another forty nine passengers landing from the "Dale Princess" - many to pause and take pictures of the most photographed razorbills in Christendom on a ledge immediately below. Some of these shots appeared in journals featuring Britain's wild fringes, but there was nothing very wild about this one!

While North Haven was the usual landing place on Skomer, this was not so on Skokholm, where such landings were rare. The old way down to the few boats that tackled Skokholm's northern shore was via the main gully. A rope, permanently in position, had eased our passage to and from sea level, holding on with one hand and lugging stores up or down with the other. It seemed likely that fewer visitors would now avail themselves of the delights of swimming from the island's only sandy beach at the bottom, or admiring the primrose tuffets at close quarters.

The new steps led down to a promontary from which the few of us who remained stranded on the island in October one year had been rescued by Breton fishermen. On the first attempt their dinghy had been swamped in North Haven proper and this low headland was deemed the only remaining possibility.

It was back up the rope for us and down the cliff, where a flight of steps would have proved very useful, but we made it. (See "Memories of Welsh Islands" for this and other adventures of those heady days when all the world was young.)

At Calf Bay I came upon a bird watching hide, also new. No birds were visible from inside, but from outside I was able to look down on a huddle of a dozen razorbills, some with eggs, and more on the sea beyond. Local herring gulls also had full clutches of mottled brown eggs on more open sites nearby.

The worn thrift sward on the end of the Neck boasted no paths, nor needed any. Tucked under a bluff of the purple Old red mudstone inter-leaved with grey calcareous strata, I came upon another cause for nostal-gia - the plank, with which we used to cross the sea-filled gully to the Stack at low tide.

This was an unfailing excitement undertaken every week with each new batch of visitors, but evidently not for many years now, to judge by the state of the plank. Both ends had rotted to pulp and lichens had colonised the surface.

12. Sea beet

To me, as a botanist, the Stack was the island Mecca, populated only by birds with no plant-eating mammals. This was where high flung surf produced succulence in otherwise non succulent species, and provided prime habitat for the monster form of buck's-horn plantain that caused such a stir among Museum taxonomists and was the subject of years of growth experiments with the various forms under a range of conditions at my base away from the island.

Gazing now at the Stack across the two intervening gullies, I saw none of those special plants, nor any of the previously abundant tree mallow, which survived only on inaccessible cliffs. Vigorous sea beet, another unable to withstand grazing, persisted, with orache, thrift and sea campion among the herring gulls.

It is sad that this crossing, like the weekly jaunt to ring shearwaters, is denied the modern generation. I was no longer at an age where I wished to walk the plank but I felt for today's youngsters who are deprived of so many of the little thrills that we enjoyed. Not all the red tape relating to the curtailment of organised expeditions can be blamed on the Nanny State. It is a necessary precaution against the new breed of greedy, unprincipled individuals, who try to prove it is someone else's fault when they suffer a mishap, and with the crazy laws that allow them to get away with it and rake in unmerited compensation.

The cliff edge path by the Devil's Teeth was closed for the 2005 summer season, because of the breeding peregrines, so I returned further inland, viewing the crowds of puffins on the waters of Peter's Bay from rocks off the South Landing.

All hands converged on the Wheelhouse at four on Tuesday afternoon - Jeffery from the de-rusting and painting of the second hand wheelbarrow which he had contributed to the island equipment on our way there, and me from the west and North Pond. The occasion was a double celebration, for Pema Marriott, one of the resident volunteers, who was twenty eight today, and Jo and David, who were announcing their engagement.

After the presents, eats and speeches the visitors learned that the weather was 'blowing up', as if it hadn't been doing that all along. If we waited until our scheduled departure on the morrow we might be marooned until the end of the week. A boat was coming to take us ashore tonight and was bringing in the parents of the happy couple to launch the family celebrations. All this was arrarranged by the new two way radio link, said to be fueled by solar and wind power.

At Martinshaven we divided forces, manhandling baggage or fetching cars from the National Trust carpark on the clifftop. Martin Payne had come to collect Irene, his gardening wife, and these good folk took us under their wing. We squeezed aboard under piles of gear and were about to drive off when accosted by the Rev. Ted, who had mislaid his luggage. It turned up on my lap!

We were too late for trains to Cardiff and Bristol and our friends offered us hospitality, which we felt was too much of an imposition. A scouring of Haverfordwest for b and bs, however, proved unsuccessful, though generating more laughs than it merited. The merriment continued all evening, as we enjoyed a delightful spell in an old farmhouse in the heart of the Prescelly Mountains.

The miles between unfolded some of rural Pembrokeshire at its best, culminating in the heathy hillsides with their wealth of ice-borne erratics littered across what must have been the famous bluestone.

As we approached the house in the gloaming a few bats flew out from the eaves. Inside were feline and canine welcomes. My brood of cats at home consists of small feral tabbies who make a convenience of me but will never be lap cats. It was good to sit, glass in hand, with a large bundle of purring fur draped across my lap. Martin got busy in the kitchen with a wok and we dined in style. Jeffery was last seen asleep on the sofa, clasping a bottle.

It was doubtful if the predicted storm materialised. Admittedly the sun drenched grounds of the farmhouse, with its big, newly excavated pond, spacious lawn and spring flowers, was a very different habitat from those windswept acres beyond the sea to be able to judge fairly.

Laughter still bubbled as we made our separate conducted tours and were finally ferried those extra delightful miles back to Haverfordwest and the civilisation that lay beyond.

A few months after our Maytime stay on Skokholm the owner of the island, Mrs. Osra Lloyd Phillips of Dale Castle, died and it became necessary for the island to be sold, to defray death duties.

13. Seagulls and sea campion

Held in medieval times by the Earl of Pembroke, Skokholm had been part of the Dale Estate since it was bought for three hundred pounds in 1646 by barrister William Phillips of Haythog. It had been leased as a bird observatory for nearly eighty years, with the exception of the war years, when it was out of bounds. The first lessee, from 1927, was Ronald Lockley, who paid a rent of twenty six pounds a year or ten shillings a week in old money.

Currently the lease was in the capable hands of the South and West Wales Wildlife Trust which, in its several guises, had held it for over fifty years, initially as the West Wales Field Society.

The unique scenery, flora and fauna, is inviolate, as an SSSI, and the executors were offering it exclusively to the trust, rather than putting it on the open market. ITV news on 5th October, 2005 announced:

"The island is to be bought for the nation at a cost of around one million pounds. It is to become as customer-friendly as Skomer, many thousands of pounds to be spent on improving amenities and transport to and from the island."

This was evocatively illustrated by a possie of grey Atlantic seals draped over rocks and rabbits gambolling on the plateau. In the event the price was £750,000.

Many thousands were currently being spent on Skomer, an island owned by the Countryside Council for Wales and managed, like Skokholm, by the Wildlife Trust. This was closed to all visitors but day trippers during the 2005 season while the building work proceeded. It seems that both islands are to become tourist honeypots.

In the post war years frugality was valued as attracting only serious science students, willing to put up with the inconveniences to avail themselves of this unique opportunity to pursue their studies. Many grew to become university lecturers, professors or life-long researchers. The first long term warden, the late Peter Conder OBE, became chief of the RSPB, which grew to have over a million members during his term of office. Skokholm was a source of recruits for the prestigious Edward Grey Institute of Ornithology at Oxford, of new theories expounded and papers published, particularly on bird migration under the tutelage of Geoffrey Matthews.

The youngsters contributed little in the way of cash, but the staff were mostly volunteers, wholly content with full board in return for their services and contributions to the growing mass of biological data. There was tremendous competition to be appointed as volunteer cook for a season, by people with a love of the wild but no biological qualifications or aspirations.

Then came a period when many visitors were more mature, with serious interests in the natural phenomena that the Pembrokeshire Islands shared with those of Scotland and Ireland, but in a more amenable climate and less remote from centres of civilisation. Day trippers and picnickers were a rarity because of landing difficulties.

Now much of the basic research has been achieved. A wider world has opened up to young hopefuls in the realms of science. Also, and not before time, the general populace has become more aware of the value of these surviving scraps of real Earth habitat.

The time is ripe for those of us who have been privileged to know this unspoiled habitat through the 'glory decades', to share its wildlife spectacle with others who realise its worth. The more folk who range themselves against the wholesale destruction of the natural world, that has overspilled its bounds in our greed to extract ever more from our planet's limited resources, the better.

If large numbers are to have the opportunity to visit these prime sites at first hand, large resources must be employed to safeguard what they have come to see. Warden Jo appeared on the TV item saying "We have no electricity or hot running water." Few had ever dreamed that there should be such amenities in such a place, but time marches on.

When supermarkets instead of the local rabbits, goats and gulls are provisioning the establishment, more and more cash must be contributed by visitors, and they are likely to expect such frills in this demanding modern age. "Memories of Welsh Islands" documented the past sixty years. The next sixty will be very different.

ADDENDUM

Another Skokholm visit was planned for the 2nd August, 2006 - "A Skokholm Day Founders' Meeting" - to celebrate completion of the purchase of the island by the Wildlife Trust. Sadly the weather was against us, as on my visits to English and Irish islands in May and June, but those we managed to achieve, Skokholm we did not.

On arrival in Pembrokeshire we learned that a force five wind would prevent so large a gathering being ferried across to the island. Instead we crowded into the inadequately small Marloes Village Hall.

14. The north coast, Skokholm

Ironically the sun blazed down from an almost cloudless sky, as it had done through most of the previous month, July 2006 being the hottest July since records began, with temperatures commonly in the 80s Fahrenheit, nudging the nineties. The drought was expected to match that of 1976, but August was cool and damp throughout.

Many of the standing crowd failed to see the speakers over the forest of heads and most fought their way out into the sunshine with their buffet lunch. There followed an exodus to the nearest cliffs, where we shared nostalgic views of the island with the plump, self satisfied ponies grazing the clifftop sward of the Old Deer Park.

There she lay, serene upon the blue vault - purple-red cliffs topped by a yellowing greensward, her destiny hopefully now secure for all time. A number of other sailings had had to be cancelled during the rumbustious gales of May and June now that the boat left from Martinshaven to negotiate the notorious Jack Sound instead of from Dale Fort as in the past. If the weather men are right there may be more disappointments.

Nevertheless, the lure of the islands is as strong as ever. Following a TV programme by Iolo Williams featuring them, three hundred people turned up for the next early boat out to Skomer. Although much larger than in the early days - a capacious fifty seater - two hundred and fifty still had to be turned away!

Thanks once again to the generosity of my good friends, Irene and Martyn Payne, in their Prescelly Mountain stronghold, I was more than compensated by the ensuing days exploring the splendid cliffs and spacious beaches of the Pembrokeshire Coast National Park and the mossy, bouldery mountain woodland of Ty Canol near the Pentre Isaf Cromlech - a National Nature Reserve with four hundred species of lichen, a dragonfly pool and, surely, a population of elves to boot.

2
Cape Clear, Co. Cork
AN ISLAND BIRD OBSERVATORY

I had recently returned from my wanderings in the Southern Hemisphere, to settle in South Wales and had become the proud owner of my first car. A lover of winding lanes rather than screeching highways, I decided to try her out in the Emerald Isles. It was a little unnerving seeing her swung aboard the Irish ferry by crane at Fishguard, three chocks fixed around each wheel, also backing her down the ramp from the railway wagon on which she had achieved her first short passage in Rosslare, but the miles to come were delightful.

There was a long term bus strike on at the time - April, 1963 - and I had the roads almost to myself, just walkers, cyclists, a few donkey carts and plodding beasts with panniers. It was exactly right for bird watching at a leisurely pace. This was the season of the spring migration, with far more birds arriving or passing through than I had seen on my drive down through Wales.

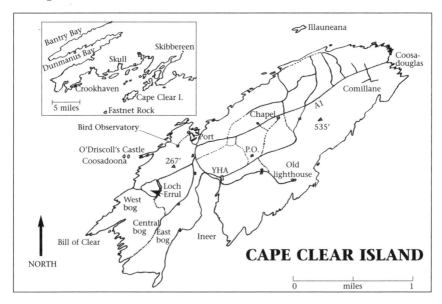

Both species of martin had arrived and I watched a hooded crow scraping the corpse of a rat from the road. Curlews bubbled, a bittern boomed and flocks of finches and larks came rollicking past. No wonder the Bird Observatory of Saltee Island in the South-east, equidistant between Wexford and Waterford Harbours, had been able to record so many unusual bird species during the past decade.

Keeping off the highways where possible, the two hundred and twenty six miles to Baltimore provided plenty of opportunities for going astray, but there was usually someone to ask.

"Maudlinstown? Oh we call that Wellington Bridge." So did the signposts, but not the map. "Tis a mile from here. An Irish mile, mind you!".

Lost in a maze of villages where signposts were in short supply, I accosted an elderly couple. "Where am I?"

They looked at me in bewilderment, pointing at the patch of Mother Earth on which they stood. "Why, you're here of course."

How could anyone not know the hamlet where they had spent their entire lives?

Cutting across the heads of various estuaries, where waders poked around the mudflats, I arrived in Baltimore on the morning of the third day and was directed to a cheery little old man loafing on the quay.

He proved to be the mate of the "Puffin", a small open boat which plied to and from Cape Clear Island when the larger mail ferry was not running. "Puffin" seemed an optimistic name, as these inimitable birds were rare on Cape Clear, with only thirty pairs breeding in 1963 - these down to a mere ten pairs by 1969.

"Puffin", the boat, was owned by one of the islanders and supplemented the ferry during busy periods in summer when that had more would-be passengers than could be accommodated. Leaving my car in the boatyard, I set sail at two thirty pm, with just two others. These were island women who had come ashore to do their monthly shopping, both having walked three miles across the island to catch the boat. A month's stores can get very heavy in that distance on the homeward trek.

Not everyone lived near the quay. The island was three miles (5 km) long and up to one mile (c2 km) wide, occupying 1,578 acres and rising to 553 feet at Knockcaranteen.

"Puffin" wove a course through a number of delightful offshore islands and sundry sea-birds, including small flocks of black guillemots or tysties, which we do not see as far south as this in England and Wales. We rounded the north end of Sherkin Island, the largest, proceeding towards Hera Island, then south-west to run along the north shore of

Cape Clear Island. Clouds lay heavy over the mainland, but Clear was living up to its name. The sky could not have been bluer, nor the rugged cliffscape more sharply defined. Scattered, it seemed at random, were the dots of land known as Carberry's Hundred Isles rising above the waves.

Sherkin and Clear Islands form the south-eastern arm of Roaringwater Bay - which was not living up to its fearsome name today. Three and a half miles beyond them, in the same alignment to the south-west, is Fastnet Rock - that name so familiar from the twice daily radio shipping bulletins. "Lundy and Fastnet" pinpointed all that was happening weatherwise off South-west Ireland. Lundy I had known since 1954, when its self-appointed 'king', Martin Coles Harman, had reigned supreme. Fastnet I would be able to approach no closer than this.

The three islands, Sherkin, Clear and Fastnet, are the peaks of a submerged peninsula leading back through Baltimore to Skibbereen.

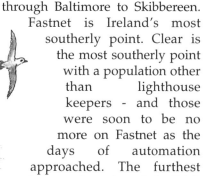

15. Fulmars off the Fastnet Rock

Fastnet is Ireland's most southerly point. Clear is the most southerly point with a population other than lighthouse keepers - and those were soon to be no more on Fastnet as the days of automation approached. The furthest south-westerly point of the Irish mainland is Mizen Head, withstanding ceaseless bombardment by Atlantic rollers a few miles further west.

Up to the end of the previous decade there had been bird observatories on Ireland's three other corners - at Saltee, Copeland in the north-east and Tory Island in the north-west but none in the south-west. The advance party of ornithologists who came to reconoitre on Clear Island, from mid August to late November in 1959, was wholly satisfied with the records they had managed to accumulate.

As well as the expected coastal birds there was good opportunity for sea watching, telescopes revealing pelagic ocean wanderers, such as skuas on the way to their Scottish nesting islands, that are usually missed, and enabling the experts to identify shearwater species other than the resident Manx.

Big flocks of autumn migrants were commuting from both north and south and they spotted no less than seventeen extremely rare species. It left them in no doubt that this was an ideal site in which to complete the four square coverage of bird movements.

Sadly, the Saltee Bird Observatory in the South-east, which had opened in 1950, had to be closed in 1963 due to a combination of difficulties, but not before a great deal of information had been acquired. At the time the east coast passage of migrating birds was regarded by the experts as much busier than that of the West, but the Cape Clear findings showed that vagrants from continental Europe were straying a lot further west than was formerly thought.

When a very suitable house was put up for sale at Ineermore, the group was unable to muster the necessary three hundred pounds and it was bought by the Irish Youth Hostels Association. The founding committee was offered the alternative of "Stroma" in Lissamona, an inconveniently long way up the wearisome hill climbed by the island's main road, the M1.

16. *Clear Island Youth Hostel.*

The bird work was based here for the three years of 1960, 61 and 62, when the much more appropriate Harbour House became available. Birders moved in, lock, stock and barrel, in March 1963 and were securely installed when I arrived a month later in April.

Speeding along under Cape Clear's northern bastions, we were not too close to the forbidding cliffs to see the plateau beyond. The cottages were scattered right across the patchwork of green pastures and black moorland, just as I had seen others a year or so before on Fair Island, between Orkney and Shetland.. There was no gathering together into villages, but the northen port, with its three pubs, known locally as 'the stations of the cross', was the hub of activities.

This was hidden until our trim little craft, with scarlet gunwhale, tall mast and tiny deck cabin, turned into the long inlet, bounded to port by dark cliffs. Vertically aligned strata presented a vertical face to the water, pierced by a dark, forbidding cave. To starboard the terrain was more

17. *"Puffin" leaves harbour*

jumbled, with moss-smooth domes of thrift and spreads of white scurvy grass.

As we slid smoothly into the little harbour the new observatory stood proud, and as sprucely whitewashed as any Trinity House light-house. Harbour House was deservedly regarded as the smartest of any on the island - where blown salt spray took a heavy toll of all structures. Folk were drifting down to the landing, as is the way on islands when a boat arrives, but sea-going activities had dwindled of late and the area was usually deserted at low water, when boats lolled high and dry on the sand or leaned askew against the harbour walls.

With the sinewy seaman who greeted our arrival was a little red pony cart, pulled by a skewbald horse. Maybe the two shopping ladies would get a lift with their purchases. Beyond the capstan to which we made fast was an elongated stack of cylindrical lobster pots. Their straight sides were of parallel wooden lathes, held by circular hoops, and their ends of rope netting. Here were none of the domes of inbent withies nor the plastic replicas of subsequent years.

Their ballast was lumps of concrete, as though the owners could find no handy rocks! Further inland, against a smoke-blackened, smooth-faced wall holding up the grassy slope behind, was an old oil drum beside a blackened fireplace. This was where the fishing nets were tarred to make them more seaworthy. Just beyond was a sturdy clump of New Zealand flax *(Phormium colensoi)*, its leaf tips dry and tattered, from a mixture of tarry smoke and salty spray.

18. *New Zealnad Flax*

Great mounds of tarred nets, with only slightly lighter coloured floats, were piled along another solid rock quay with two trawlers moored

40

alongside, black hulled, red decked and with small deck houses not much larger than "Puffin's". One of the mounds of net was being paid out and hauled aboard by two navy-clad figures, to be folded neatly on deck, ready for going over the side.

A narrow lane led off up the valley, lined with mounded banks of golden gorse, beckoning the newcomer into the interior. This followed the 'waist' of the island, which separated the larger northern block from the more rugged and various "Western Townland" or Ballyieragh.

Eighteen year old Peter Wright was one of those meeting "Puffin" this afternoon. He had just started a three month spell as temporary warden between leaving school in Cambridge and starting university in Bangor in North Wales, where he would be reading botany and ecology. In later years he joined the staff of the Nature Conservancy Council as a full time ecologist.

The other in residence throughout my all too short week here was Ham Kenney, a seasoned bird-watcher from Dublin, who had been here several times before. He became my self appointed and invaluable guide, enhancing the sights and sounds of this intriguing wildscape with a wealth of Irish stories. Virginia van der Belt, our third member, was fresh from three year's teaching in New Zealand, where I had taught in Palmerston North University for a year, and we got on famously, but she left a few days after my arrival.

Close to our living quarters were the picturesque ruins of St. Kieran's twelfth or thirteenth century church, St. Kieran, the patron saint, said to have been born here in AD 352. The roofless side walls of the knave were topped with the lemon-yellow flowers of kidney vetch, the end one with a creeping mat of red English stonecrop. Sundry gravestones protruded from the unkempt turf within. The slit window at the opposite end under its curved arch of stone flags showed the thickness of the walls.

In the elevated alcove of a separate edifice a white statue of the Virgin Mary kept an eye on things, an acolyte kneeling at a lower level. Mounted in front was the weather-worn, erect, lichen-daubed St. Kieran's

19. *The Shrine of St Kerian by the harbour*

41

Stone, sometimes referred to as a cross, but having only a few striations on its surface.

After a preliminary potter around the little port, with its imposing memorial stones surmounted by Celtic crosses in the waterside grave-yard, Ham led me away on an exploratory walkabout past a row of fishermen's cottages with Arum lilies romping round their doorways. The several locals met en route were the best possible adjunct to getting the feel of the place before starting to assess the various plant communities and list species.

One was the island poet, a wizened little man, bones protruding from the long, narrow face which typified most of the island men seen. Many had spare frames and far-seeing blue eyes and looked either undernourished or overworked or both, though the women were more buxom. Was the similarity the result of inbreeding or of the harsh environment, suffered more by the men at sea than the women in the fields and the kitchens?

The domestic set-up in the Observatory was quite basic in those early days, all participants mucking in with chores, as on Skokholm and many another such island emporium. This obviously bothered me very little, as no reference was made to the daily menage in the log of my stay.

Quite early in our walk we came to the priest's house, a local landmark. The young priest greeted us with a "Good evening", the standard comment if midday had passed.

"You get slower and slower on this island" quoth he. "Time is no object. Meals when you think about them. Tea at any time up to eleven pm unless somebody chivvies. We get our own breakfast and lunch, about three pm, or take it out."

Peter, the warden, had only been here for two days, so perhaps his timetable would be less elastic. The priests, it seemed, were moved on every few years, lest they become too lackadaisical, or yearn for a wider range of parishioners.

Our next encounter was with an elderly farmer, who lamented the dwindling of the population. In his youth there were two schools, one for boys and one for girls, with about a hundred in each. Now there were only thirty five pupils and one schoolmaster - who must have had his work cut out catering for a range of ages simultaneously. About eight hundred people lived here when our informant was at school, now there were only two hundred and forty.

A thriving mackerel fishery had been the mainstay of the islanders then. Two hundred women had been employed cleaning the fish in the harbour before the bulk was sent off to America.

"Now the Americans have got the method of fishing them for themselves, and that finished us! There was also a knitting facory, but all the girls left. Can't get young people to stay."

There seemed quite a lot of ginger-haired, freckle-faced cherubs about at the time, buxom, rosy cheeked youngsters like those one sees growing up in the ferocious gales of the Outer Hebrides or ski-ing to school in the Alps.

Here, as elsewhere on our Atlantic fringes, farmers could not be just farmers any longer, even in the early 1960s, but needed another source of income. Their need arose from having little land and few animals. Mainland English and Welsh farmers with far more of both are not much better off in the new millennium, stifled by red tape and middlemen taking more than their share of the profits, but they would seem like millionaires to those struggling island husbandmen of the mid twentieth century.

Some gained a living on Cape Clear as publicans, storekeeper or postmistress. Men who once ran their own boats might crew for other skippers based further afield. Many had joined the merchant navy during the war and numbers had not built up again since.

The diminutive elderly postman whom we met further on covered many miles afoot, dragging a long suffering donkey laden with mail and stores brought in by the ferry. He supplemented his wages by hiring out the island's few tractors. At that time there were only two cars on Cape Clear, one of them the priest's, lacking its full complement of wheels, its back axle supported by rocks.

Most ploughing, and certainly harrowing and lighter jobs, were dependent on horse power. Horse, donkey and mule might be teamed together to pull the heavier implements and we also encountered the less usual hinny, the sire a horse stallion and the dam a mare donkey, jennet or jenny. This is the opposite cross to the one producing a mule. The brown, medium sized hinnies

20. Donkey and Hinny

43

were regarded as being stronger than donkeys and less bad tempered than mules, but birthing could be a problem with the dam so much smaller than the sire, so they are a rarity. There were plenty of light work horses about still, of all coat colours, including piebald and skewbald.

Most of the old people seemed to be financed by younger ones who had gone elsewhere to earn a living, this in spite of our informant's comment:

"They make a lot of money. And spend it, too!"

Many formerly went to America, but increasingly more were heading to England by the middle of the twentieth century. In later years children over twelve years old were sent to boarding school on the mainland and were unlikely to want to return to their natal land, except, perhaps, in old age, when the delights and defects of the big wide world outside paled, and they developed a nostalgic yearning for the old time peace of child-hood years.

Most of the holdings had a cow or cows for milk, these over-wintered on turnips and hay, but shortage of winter feed necessitated most of the calves arriving in spring when the grass began to grow. A young calf sold for around twelve pounds. If kept for a few years to full size, they might bring eighty pounds into the family coffers.

Goats were kept by some for milk and possibly a pig for pork and bacon, but I saw no sheep in my wanderings. The light draught horses were used for haulage as well as cultivations and we were introduced to one that was thirty four years old and enjoying a well earned retirement. We also met an aged donkey who spent most of his time between feeds "stretched" on the ground - he too, past serving his master. All the animals encountered were very forthcoming, evidently regarding humans as friends. Or did they know that the likes of us, furnished with binoculars, were unlikely to put them to work?

In this, the spring of the year, the free range geese had goslings, the ducks ducklings and the hens chicks. Turkeys were fattening up for the festive season and guinea fowl filling their role as watchdogs, warning the rest of approaching strangers.

Much of the island was untended, the husbanded plots serving mostly as pasturage and for occasional hay crops. Arable land was rarer, most growing the traditional Irish potatoes. Carrots would have been appreci-ated but rabbits appreciated them as well and were too successful in getting in first.

Many of the 'tatties' had been planted four rows together, as on a miniature lazy bed, instead of in single rows. An old man digging out furrows between each set commented:

"Loosening the soil, ready for later earthing up."

A few fields sprouted spring-sown cereals and there were seedling Brassicas, which might evolve into cabbage, kale, turnip or swede as they matured.

Soil waterlogging necessitated late planting of crops - this a factor mitigating also against the general use of tractors puddling the ground, as well as did the small size of the fields. An average holding was probably around ten acres, criss-crossed by walls, construction of which was the most convenient means of getting rid of the loose rocks removed to make plots farmable.

Cottages on the whole seemed more commodious than the average 'black house' of a Hebridean crofter at that time. They were built of local stone, with mud used as mortar, and sometimes an external layer of plastering, Devon cob style. Roofs were mostly thatched, with cereal straw, reeds or even heather from the bogs. Ropes of twisted straw thrown across them with rocks tied to their ends kept the thatch from blowing away. Some were derelict and there was a trend for slate or corrugated iron for new roofs as the old houses were converted to barns and replacements built.

Next day the sun blazed down again from a cloudless sky, its heat diminished by the brisk sea breeze, so that we got more sunburnt than we believed possible in such comfortable temperatures. Ham and I set off after breakfast to explore the rugged western headlands, meeting up with Peter and Virginia to eat our sandwiches around two o'clock and then going our own ways until seven thirty, when we converged again on tinned corn beef and home-grown spuds. In the morning we concentrated on birds. In the afternoon I set about my botanical survey, to give a rather grand title to what I was able to achieve in the short time available.

21. Purple Sandpipers

It was early in the season yet for the auks to come ashore, but there were goodly flocks of razorbills and guillemots rafting on the sea. We saw only a single puffin but the little groups of black and white tysties were a delight and more than made up for this. Shags were ranged along sea level rocks, sinister black silhouettes

45

outlined against the shimmering sea. Cormorants and oyster catchers were fewer but there were plenty of fulmars and kittiwakes on and around the steep cliffs. A small flock of hard-to-see purple sandpipers sorted through brown seaweeds exposed by the tide and offshore were the distant black forms of scoter riding the gentle swell.

Trekking through the heather we spotted a kestrel - swooping down a rocky slope not much more than a foot from the ground - a falcon, her barred tail spread. She disappeared ino a crevice and we moved in closer after twenty minutes to investigate. As she slipped quietly away she revealed a new nest of heather and grass tufts with no eggs as yet. There were two ways out under the rock overhang. We beat a hasty retreat and it was not long before she returned. Neither peregrine falcon nor sparrow hawk, both resident, showed themselves today.

A handsome cock reed bunting was singing his heart out in an eastern reed bed, but we failed to spot his mate. Perhaps she was on eggs. This was the place where a short-eared owl, probably passing through, had been seen a day or two before. The unmistakable and now seldom heard call of a cuckoo came wafting across the heather. That, too, may have been headed elsewhere, but a few stayed to breed at that time, parasitising the meadow pipits.

Mallard, teal and moorhens were put up from some of the little ponds. Stonechats, formerly the most abundant small passerines on the island, had suffered badly everywhere during the horrendous frosts of the early 1960s, so it was very satisfying to see a pair busily feeding away on their respective dung heaps in the corner of a field.

Apparently the spring migration was drawing to a close now, but there were still some newcomers. We managed to approach very close to an exhausted song thrush pecking frantically into the turf. No live lapwings were seen, but we were able to count several score corpses. This species had suffered particularly badly during those winters. Moving west from Europe, over England and Wales to Ireland, there was nowhere else to go for the winter flocks beyond these south-western peninsulas. There had not been much snow here, but the last had been a particularly bitter winter, followed by a wet spring and many died of hunger and exhaustion.

One of the dead lapwings picked up two months before had been ringed as a pullus in Norway, so they were moving south as well as west. In more normal winters far fewer birds bother to move this far west.

A bedraggled snipe corpse lay in a bog pool, but we saw a few live ones too, probing those amazingly long bills into soggy peat. Curlew were also about, often audible, occasionally visible. Corncrakes would be around later in the year. It was early yet for them. This diminishing species was seldom recorded then in Eastern Ireland.

22. *Snipe*

Corvids were about, represented by species which we seldom see, while carrion crows and rooks were not to be expected. Ravens cronked their way across the sky, emitting three throaty notes in succession on each downward swoop of an undulating flight. A single pair of jackdaws was nesting on the cliffs near the observatory. Hoodies were common breeders on cliff ledges and were notorious egg thieves. Pick of the bunch were the choughs, and these were quite common. They moved around in groups, squealing their uncrowlike calls, and were seen every day. One of the ragamuffin ravens, which may have been in a fight, or was it moulting, had wing tips as widely splayed as the chough's. Magpies, surprisingly, with so few trees, were not infrequent, but there were no jays.

Starlings and house sparrows were as familiar as around larger farmyards on the mainland and other garden passerines were robin, blackbird and dunnock. Wheatears had been among the first of the migrants to take up territories on the moorlands, along with the ever present rock and meadow pipits, but Ham said more pairs were arriving daily, filling the gaps between the first comers.

A skylark was trilling a soft sub-song from a stone gatepost. Yellowhammers and greenfinches perched on gorse sprigs in the absence of intersecting hedgerows. Would that we could see more of these dashing yellow buntings nowadays. Many linnets had wintered here in their summer quarters, but we watched a flock migrating through. Chaffinches, once among our commonest birds, had been badly hit by toxic chemicals in Eire as well as the UK and had not been seen here yet this year.

"Willow:chiffs" and a lone goldcrest were spied in an Escallonia hedge by a cottage, but we saw no tits. A pair of pied wagtails entertained us, the cock running towards his intended with quick, mincing steps, shoulders hunched and feathers fluffed, only to be rebuffed by the flighty hen.

Genuine rock doves, small dove-grey birds with white rumps, were nesting quite commonly around the cliffs. Stock doves were present, but fewer. These have no white rump and resemble a smaller version of a wood pigeon (not present here) but without the white neck patches that give the larger bird its alternative name of ring dove.

If we had any doubts that spring had arrived, these were dispelled by the not infrequent passing of swallows. Both martin species were among them, but there were no swifts as yet. The belief at that time was that Cape Clear was not on the main migration routes, those following the east and west coasts of the Irish Sea rather than moving this far west. Ringing was establishing that most birds coming this way were from Spain, but there was an east-west migration of skylarks wintering on the west coast and nesting in Germany. It may have been some of those that thronged in Cardiff city gardens, dying in the snow, during those recent bitter winters.

Such was the sunshine on that spring day that we were able to watch several lizards soaking up its rays before launching into the business of

23. common Lizard

summer. Rats were present on the island, and mice, the latter said to be mainly in the houses.

Rabbits were abundant, apparently less affected, if at all, by the Myxomatosis that had hit the mainland population, but they had not been much exploited by the islanders since the general outbreak. The island conies were smaller than usual, as often on islands where uninhibited numbers compete for the same meagre supply of winter food. They seemed to be a brighter brown than usual, or was that the sunshine picking out their highlights? There were few, if any, of the blacks, whites and skewbalds sometimes found on islands.

After the lunch rendezvous I sought out my favourite habitat of clifftops, where the birds impinging on my consciousness were mainly gulls. Herring gulls were mating, the males trying to balance atop the females with much wing flapping and no recourse to grabbing her by the scruff of the neck to steady themselves, as the drake mallard were doing while half drowning their mates on the big ponds. Sometimes the hen bird would call softly throughout, mimicking the supplicating "more more" call of a hungry chick.

A greater black-back, up to its hocks in water, was doing battle with something large, flabby and fishy, raising a goodly splash in the doing. Constantly shaking its burden like a terrier with a rat, it tugged at it, taking a few steps backwards but without detaching a swallowable morsel. The expedient adopted by crows, parrots, even tits, of holding the prey with one foot in order to detach a handy sized chunk, seemed not to have occurred to it.

I came upon a veritable cornucopia of expectorated crop pellets revealing a wide range of food items. On other sites it was usually possible to recognise individual feeding habits, the contents of each coughed up feeding package composed of the same prey remains, and aggregations of pellets likewise. Here there was a right mix-up, as though birds had to seek far and wide to fill their crop.

There were a lot of corn pellets, most of the grain removed but the discarded chaff recognisable as that of barley, the most cultivated cereal on the island. April was far from harvest time. Had they been pillaging the stored grain or gleaning in fields not yet sown to spring crops?

Fish bones, fragments of crab legs and bits of the aerated internal skeletons of cuttlefish were sometimes mixed with the chaff. Smashed and whole shells of mussels, periwinkles and even limpets were found. Perhaps the gulls had learned how to prise the latter from their usual tight hold on the rocks during the recent frosts, when the molluscan muscles had lost their ability to cling on. Pellets were almost as frequent by pools of water dominated by dwarf sea plantain, as they were in the habitual gull gathering grounds on worn turf of buck's horn plantain and fescue.

Anthills were frequent where the ground was sufficiently dry. In limey country the plants they support may stand out from the rest because lime leaches from the loosened, raised soil, leading to a more acid vegetation on the mounds. Here it seemed to be the humic acids that were leaching out, leading to a less acid-loving flora atop the anthills. Bird's foot trefoil had a good footing here, along with knotted pearlwort and upstanding Cladonia lichens - while all about were Scottish heather, the two common heaths and western gorse.

24. Bird's-foot trefoil

That, unfortunately, was the end of the sunny spell. During the next few days we were immersed in a clammy cloud of mirky mist, dark as bilge water. Call it what we would, it dampened our ardour and caused the cameras to be left behind. Virginia departed on the nine o'clock ferry.

I explored the narrow peninsulas west of the harbour, finishing up at Coosadoona, the imposing hollow ruin of O'Driscoll's Castle. Its headland seemed to have been recently separated from the main island, still accessible at low water but quite a scramble to get there.

Some of the islanders still bore the name of O'Driscoll. He who the castle was named for, like Marisco of Lundy Island out across the southern sea, was a notorious pirate, adept at intercepting ships sailing the trade routes home, laden with bounty. There was a certain pride in bearing so infamous a name, akin to that of Australians who boast their ancient lineage in that continent by claiming convicts as their forebears.

The mist settled, steamy and breathless, where little waves lapped on the stones, but the stillness onshore was absolute. These sometimes tranquil places had been the abode of holy men, as well as pirates and malefactors

The massed twin heads of kidney vetch on rocky ridges overshadowed drifts of white scurvy grass flowers in the gullies below. Primroses and violets snuggled in sheltered depressions, some among stunted sloe bushes not much taller. Ubiquitous springtime celandines glistened through globules of condensed fog and Oxalis wood sorrel, template for the Irish shamrock, had strayed from woodland to raise shy blooms among tuffets of hardier thrift. Little mauve 'snapdragons' of ivy-leaved toadflax scrambled up the flanks of narrow headlands, which were more or less aligned with those projecting from the island's extreme south-west.

These rocky ribs seemed to dominate the landscape throughout. As in much of South-west Ireland, the basal rock type is Devonian Old Red Sandstone, but not as homogeneous as that of Skokholm. It embraces a complicated mix of shales and slates with quartzite intrusions.

The dip of the rocks throughout is between seventy and eighty degrees, the strata of some appearing almost vertical. They form the flank of a great fold in the Earth's crust - the result of mountain building pressure from the south-east. Incessant wave action has eroded out narrow inlets between the ribs at each end of the island, these associated with caverns and blow holes.

Before accumulation of the superficial peat, much of the bedrock was covered by glacial drift and there are morainic deposits around the harbour, the material transported either by ice or ancient rivers. Soil generally is infertile, often podsolized, with impermeable iron pans or clay pans. Most is quite shallow above the bedrock and the drier peats can be fragmentary above the podsols, but there are thicker, more glutinous accumulations in the bogs.

The peat, however, is insufficient to supply fuel to the populace, although we spotted a few narrow-bladed, peat-digging spades with foot rest on one side only. Coal had to be imported and, in the absence of trees, the poorer people might be reliant on bracken and furze for cooking and warmth. These, if stored in the rafters, were a fire hazard. In fact many people, it seemed, wintered on the mainland, where there was a better chance of keeping the cold at bay and the tatties on the boil. They returned when the pockets of more fertile brown earths dried sufficiently to give a tilth suitable for ploughing and harrowing.

Moving back from outcrops where lichens were crisp underfoot into zones with less naked rock, the rough grassland was speckled with the pale blue of thyme leaved speedwell and darker blue of heath milkwort, with more sombre flecks of field and heath woodrush sprinkled with yellow pollen sacs. Mauve ground ivy and Danish scurvy grass clothed small patches to the exclusion of most else, barren strawbery and hairy bitter cress were less pushy.

Most exciting in this community were little clumps of Irish spurge *(Euphorbia hyberna)*, which is seldom found in the UK outside the area for which it is named. The acid yellow flower heads are on show from April to July, to be followed by warty cylindrical fruits.

25. *Irish spurge*

This is one of Ireland's few Lusitanian species, centred in Spain and Portugal. Here it is concentrated on these south-western peninsulas and its rare occurrences in the UK are in similar coastal sites of Devon and Cornwall. I came across it later bordering lanes and it seemed to be quite common on Cape Clear, as is the only other representative of the Lusitanian flora.

That is the pale butterwort *(Pinguicula lusitanica)*, an insectivorous plant of wet flushes and the low banks of streams. More widespread than the other, this inhabits the Atlantic fringes of Cornwall, Ireland and Scotland but seems to miss out on Wales, although

26. *Pale Butterwort*

growing across the Irish Sea in South-east Eire. The violet shaped flowers are an anaemic mauve compared with those of the more dashing common butterwort and the insect-catching leaves are a bluish rather than yellowish green. The magnificent great butterwort is a speciality of South-west Ireland but had not been found on Cape Clear.

Ham and I sallied forth on a seven mile walkabout on the north island block after lunch, side-stepping around livestock wandering the lanes. The sea mist was as thick as ever, the land like a sepia photo, so no views were to be had. Birds were skulking, as is their wont in early afternoon, so we focussed on plants.

Wall flora was sparse, despite the proliferation of walls bounding the mosaic of tiny fields. With neither timber nor iron available the gateways were partially blocked by piles of loose rocks after the livestock had been let through.

A farmer looming out of the mist said that these functioned as a psychological barrier rather than a real one. Horses and donkeys could certainly have clambered over some, although cattle are less adventurous. On the mainland hunters and hacks that fly gracefully over hedges with a rider on their back and a pack of hounds ahead, can often be seen grazing quietly in paddocks with boundaries less formidable but evidently respected as the edge of the home territory.

Some walls were little more substantial than the gates. When we queried the number of holes between loosely stacked rocks, we were told that if winds were unable to get through they might well blow them over! On the adjacent mainland some walls consisted of recurring tripods of large rock slabs with smaller ones piled between, leaving holes almost big enough to function as lamb creeps. What seemed like a line of gravestones stretching across unfarmed moorland on the island proved to be the well spaced skeleton of a wall on previously farmed land. Very likely the smaller rocks between had been re-used to build a new cottage when the old one was relegated to barn status.

If there were many rocks to be removed from a field, which could be no larger than a third of an acre, the average size being less than one acre, the walls might be more substantial. Many tell only of the agricultural past, when there were twelve hundred farmer fishermen in residence a hundred years or so earlier. We were told that only about eighty houses were still occupied, with few trawlers going to sea now to keep the men in work.

Also it was said, that walls numbered over sixteen thousand erected by gnarled hands helped by donkeys to haul the stones around on sleds.

Most were about a metre high, some almost twice this and those around houses were often reinforced by wind breaks of Fuchsia or Escallonia, which last is also a favourite on the windy Scillies. Some hedgeline Hebes have escaped to spring up on the cliffs. A few sycamores and hawthorns persist and wispier, less effective tamarisks. It is in these hedges that the ornithologists find most small birds availing themselves of the sparse shelter before moving on.

En route we passed some real 'standing stones' or gallauns, said to have a religious significance. Four in line had smaller ones between and one was pierced by a hole, through which young lovers might join hands during the marriage ceremony, to bring good fortune on their future lives together. The functional chapel is nearby, in part of the Eastern Townland and three hundred feet above sea level.

Emerging from its dim interior, after admiring the twelve stations of the cross depicted around its walls, and the attractive wood carvings, we encountered another local. He took one look at our binoculars and came out with:

"If it's birds ye're afther ye should have been here in the winter. They plovers. They was dyin' all over the place." We would scarcely have needed binoculars for those.

After a few cracks about St. Patrick, he embroidered the tale of the mackerel fishery for the Americans and waxed lyrical about the old sailing ships that called first here to drop the mail and then sailed primly on to London or Liverpool. He had just acquired some of the new issue of Irish postage stamps from the little post office. They illustrated ears of corn.

"Even postmistress was afther not knowing what the corn had to do with posting."

The patchwork of gorse, heather, rough grass or bracken was largely dependent on local shelter, spray blowing right across the whole in winter. Although bracken was safely below ground when the storms were fiercest, this occupied the most sheltered zones. Lousewort, tormentil and lesser skullcap peeped up among the heathers and splaying clumps of deer sedge *(Trichophorum caespitosum)*, and rosettes of freckled leaves heralded a crop of heath spotted orchids.

A much more varied flora grew in waterlogged parts, golden saxifrage and lady's smock being among the few already in flower. The silky white tops of the bog cotton had yet to mature from the nondescript sedge-brown flowers, and the orange-yellow spikes of bog asphodel from among the flattened, sideways tilted leaves.

Brookweed *(Samolus valerandi)* provided a maritime touch among creeping bog pimpernel and velvet-leaved marsh St. John's wort. Round-

27. Bladderwort

leaved sundew, bedded down in soggy patches of Sphagnum moss, was harvesting unwary flies on its sticky leaves. A third insectivore in the bog pools was the much rarer bladderwort, catching its prey in little underwater bladders, with lids triggered to trap unwary water fleas or Cyclops that passed too close.

Soon the tousled white flowers of bogbean and yellow Irises would be brightening the bog pools, with purple loosestrife, ragged robin, marsh cinquefoil and marsh woundwort to follow. The various mints would be the last to flower, among sporing heads of royal fern and shrubby creeping willow, topping the plethora of pondweeds.

Ivy-leaved water crowfoot wove through fool's watercress below a guano-fouled bird perch. Much rarer was the other Apium, the feathery leaved lesser marshwort *(Apium inundatum).* Shoreweed *(Littorella uniflora),* a species of temporary pools, was retaining its languid submerged growth form of winter this early in the season. The list of others seen in these boggy bits was quite impressive, fog or no fog.

The clammy mist blanket enveloped us throughout the following day, but it was pleasantly mild, a soporific world in which everything slept. No wind, no sounds, no birds: the sort of day when you could curl up under a rock and go to sleep and no-one would be any the wiser.

I pottered all morning on neatly rabbit-mown turf of sea plantain, a growth form of the plant characteristic of spray-washed cliffs in the west but seldom seen elsewhere. Sea plantain for most of us sends its six to eight inch long succulent leaves and flower spikes splaying up through sea Aster, sea lavender and sea arrow grass on salt marshes. Here the leaves seldom exceeded more than an inch long, nor attained the breadth of a matchstick, the closely packed rosettes melded into a smoothly firm but often wet turf.

As the ebb progressed I moved down into the intertidal zone in some of the little bays, where even the lapping of the waves was muted.

Seaweeds moved imperceptibly in the shallows, whispering together, small ones hidden in the folds of large. I was surprised to find at the end of the afternoon, that I had recorded almost fifty different algal species.

The mid tide zone was dominated by sea thong or thongweed (*Himanthalea elongata*), the straplike branches emerging from the centre of what appeared like a rubberised baby's dummy, and with it dark red *Gigartina stellata*. This is one of the two that is eaten in these parts as Irish moss or carragheen.

Much rarer, and always exciting finds, were bunches of spongy green *Codium fragile* with forked branches. The texture was felty, the holdfast a neatly lobed boss of interwoven filaments and the bulk greater than that of any other of our green seaweeds and much sought after by hungry molluscs. Codium species are centred further south on Mediterranean shores and are confined to the South and West in our islands.

28. Codium

Attractive waving fronds of *Alaria esculenta* swayed elegantly where wave action was brisker on the little headlands, the puckered flanges of the metre long fronds gathered into a flexible midrib. This one is eaten in Scotland under the name of tang.

Pink crusts of Lithothamnion floored upshore pools where transparent shrimps and inch long fish flitted incessantly. The familiar blue-beaded maroon beadlet anemones *(Actinia equina)* characterised this zone. More elegant snakelocks anemones *(Anemonia sulcata)* with pink tips to the undulating green tentacles were based further downshore.

The "limpet island flora" was very apparent here This term is used when the common flimsy green algae, Ulva and Enteromorpha, grow only on the shells of limpets. These conical shellfish graze the spores and young plants off the rocks when on their high water foraging expeditions, but do not feed over each others backs, so only the spores alighting there can thrive unmolested.

The muddy sand of the harbour yielded lugworms *(Arenicola marina)* in U shaped burrows and more mobile, many legged ragworms *(Nereis diversicola)*, both suitable for bait, but there seemed to be little rock fishing among the locals.

Moving briskly away to loftier cliffs, I was rewarded with fine views of diving gannets. Birds gained height between dives by describing a single circle, rising rapidly before turning into the plunge. The precipitous descent was slightly corkscrewed, birds turning 180 or 360 degrees as they dropped, while the wings were still at their widest spread, perhaps in response to a turning of the fish shoal. Wings closed only at the moment of entry. With or without a fish, the birds emerged in a flurry of foam as they shook the water from wings and body before rising in a 'thermal soar' with scarcely more than a single flap of the great wings.

They were close in under the cliff and I was able to discern mackerel sized fish in the deep, clear, green water. Those seemed to be pursuing smaller fry that had attracted several shags and razorbills. The shags looped up from the surface at the beginning of each dive and the water was so translucent that I could follow their progress beneath before they emerged to juggle a four inch long fish into a suitable position for swallowing. These gannets could be 'locals' from the Little Skellig, but the prevailing drizzly, low visibility was the sort of weather that many seabirds favoured when migrating further afield.

Sunday dawned as foggy as ever and there was little let up all day, but there were more people about. Half a dozen fishing boats had come into port for the weekend and it seemed that their crews had joined the islanders in converging on the hillside church for ten thirty mass. The rest of the sabbath for most was spent indoors, imbibing stout or Guiness and being sociable. No sound of Irish jigs drifted from the various pubs, as they did on Fair Isle, where it was reels rather than jigs.

I was given to understand that many islanders lacked ready cash (or was that only when the collecting bag came round?) It seemed to worry them very little. Many lived to a ripe old age, despite poor nutrition, their often sparse frames having to go almost everywhere on foot, but doing so with due decorum to conserve energy.

Wandering round the north of the island on that sabbath morn, I spied a couple working on some newly tilled soil alongside a large, half drowned lazy bed. The man came over for a chat.

"We don't see many folk up here. Always glad to talk."

We did for a while and he returned to his labours, not even bothering to pass the gist of our conversation on to his hard working spouse, bent doggedly to the planting of seed potatoes. Maybe the ladies don't need external stimuli to keep them going. As I melted away into the fog, with visibility down to ten yards, they pressed on, undaunted, at their back-breaking task

Much of my day was spent splashing round seepages and swamps, bogs and reedbeds. There was considerable variation in the patches of vegetation, often for no very obvious reason. Sea plantain continued from the sea fringe to mingle amicably with true acid bog, as in transects which I had studied by Scottish sea lochs. Was this encouraged by acidity seeping down into saline communities, or saltiness blowing up into acid ones - or both?

Scurvy grass, the harbour plant that was the traditional anti-scorbutic of scurvy ridden sailors coming into port after long spells at sea, was growing on Sphagnum moss clumps, yet no group of plants typifies acid bogs more closely than Sphagnum.

It was rather eerie working up to the ankles in this topsy turvy mix in such restricted visibility. Right on the cliff edge at one point I glanced up to observe a string of gannets just offshore veering suddenly away from a sea girt stack looming in their path only in the nick of time. Or were they following close inshore to get their bearings?

In the brooding stillness I got quite close to many passerines, incoming migrants, who might well have wondered where they had landed up. When I reported my whitethroat sighting in the evening it proved to be the first arrival of the season, and on the very same date as the first the previous year.

29. Whitethroat on Escallonia

It took me a long time to thread my way back to the observatory through the maze of little fields, with many deviations to avoid getting over or through the collapsible walls. The morning's shipping forecast (the one applicable in our scrap of land surrounded by so much of the Atlantic where most of the weather was brewed up) had decreed that the mist would lift at twilight. It did, and soon the stars were twinkling in apparent ecstacy at being able to show off to earthlings below.

On Monday morning we woke to dazzling sunshine, but the weatherwise seaman who poked his head in through our door warned that it would last less than an hour before the clouds regathered. I took him at his word, leaving breakfast to scurry out with camera at the ready. How right he was. With the clouds came a force five wind, for which I was ill clad. Sun and clouds were playing fast and loose with each other for the rest of the day.

When almost back I came upon a pile of human bones, newly exhumed from the ancient churchyard by St. Kieran's ruins. Today was the day of the funeral and there was scant room for extra corpses in the

30. Disinterred human bones

few plots of hallowed ground where there was enough depth of soil to cover them. Each must take his turn at decent burial and then yield place to another. There were three skulls in the earth-stained pile and some rotten planks from an old coffin.

The funeral was at two pm and I sat outside the observatory with a cheese omelette and coffee in warm sunshine, watching the procession. The whole island, plus the visiting trawlermen, must have been there, but the sombrely dressed line was of men only plus a few small boys, learning the ways of their elders.

The service had been at the chapel on the hill and the procesion came plodding down the M1 to the burial ground by the sea. Peter counted a hundred and thirty people, two thirds of these following the coffin, which was carried in state on a jaunting cart pulled by the skewbald pony that had come to meet our boat. The rest fell in at the bottom of the hill.

Twelve weathered seamen headed the procession, following the coffin en route but then dropping back. The body had been brought home from exile on the mainland on Saturday and installed in the newer church for the funeral service. Each family party moved down to pay their respects to the graves of their ancestors, disinterred or otherwise, before the new entry was laid to rest. The young 'father' officiated, wearing an oblique white sash over his black robe. Soon afterwards he was seen leaving the island on "Puffin". Ham had closed the observatory curtains, in deference to the occasion and no photos were taken.

The observatory tabby was entertaining two Toms, upstairs and down, during the evening, but the young German youth hosteller failed to make contact, as arranged.

Next day was wintry, cloudy and cold, with rain setting in by late afternoon, when I returned for 'lunch'. In this, followed by 'the meal' near midnight, I was conforming with the lackadaisical routine of the previous week's "indolent Oxford undergraduates not used to fending for themselves until need drove them".

My mission today was the exploration of Lough Errul, the freshwater lake on the south-western segment near the old coastguard station. It occupied some eleven acres (four and a half hectares). Most of the island farmsteads were supplied by shallow wells, but the lough had been a vital water supply in times of drought, when the population was larger. Rainfall was less here than on the mainland, as the clouds did not have to rise over hills high enough to persuade them to drop their moisture. A few cottages now had rain water storage tanks.

In sunshine the lake was a delight, reflecting the bluest of skies. Viewed at close quarters the water was almost innocent of suspended particles, but was stained the colour of beer by peat extracts.

In places there were sandy or gravelly beaches formed from disintegration of the parent Old Red Sandstone. Herbivores coming to drink had gnawed and trampled the vegetation at their chosen 'watering holes', baring the ground for dwarf shoreweed, marsh pennywort and lesser spearwort. Elsewhere were fringes of Eleocharis spike rush, jointed rush and curled dock. Big oval leaves of bog pondweed rafted offshore, sprinkled with duckweed and threaded by flote grass.

31. Shoreweed and Floating Marshwort

Fed by surface drainage, the loch emptied via a stream with fiorin grass and water starwort. This cascaded over the western cliff into Roaringwater Bay as a tall silver ribbon, to lose itself in the ocean. Wind was sufficiently brisk today for some to be spraying back to water the cliff face plants alongside, before eventually finding its way to dilute the jellyfish medium below.

A crop more usual in Ireland at that time than in the UK was flax, the fibres used for Irish linen rather than the seeds for linseed oil. This was washed and retted around the shores of Lough Errul, whose soft, acid waters served as a scouring or cleansing agent and also had soapy or saponaceous qualities similar to those of Welsh waterside soapwort used for the washing of sheep fleeces. Rings of stones where the stems had been laid to rett could be seen just below water level.

The lake was essentially oligotrophic or poor in nutrients, with fewer water plants than in lesser pools and runnels. No fish occurred, apart from the occasional eel which managed to commute from the sea for a spell of growth in the bog pools, where some may fall prey to the odd heron. For those there are no frogs, toads, newts or freshwater fish, so they are most likely to be seen foraging around the coast. Common lizards are the only reptiles which escaped St. Patrick and these are quite freqent along Errul's shores.

Water birds are sparse, with few swans or geese. Had they, perhaps, been shot out, along with plover, snipe, partridge and pigeon, by hungry residents, although those are said to have made little use of the sea-birds or rabbits? I looked in vain among the hundred or so gulls preening on the surface for unusual species, but saw none. All were headed into the wind which ruffled the lake surface, scattering glints of light when the sun shone. They shivvered their wings to get them thoroughly wet, rocking sideways to splash their backs and straining forwards with much flapping to shake the water from their feathers, as though to take off into the wind. All I managed to flush was a drake teal skulking under the eastern shore, but I got fine views of a kestrel tiercel perched on a wall top.

Signs of past agriculture were rife, some of the old lazy beds constructed almost a metre high to drain off excess water having succumbed to drowning. I watched a mixed horse, donkey and mule team turning narrow furrows, while broader, more meticulously straight ones, slid out behind one of the postman's tractors. A mixture of straw, dung and seaweed was being ploughed in as manure.

Driftwood or 'wreck', as opposed to 'wrack', was collected but was often too riddled by teredo borers to be useful as building material other than for fencing or too soggy for fuel until thoroughly dried (not so easy in this humid climate). 1960's fuel was mostly bottled gas, paraffin or imported coal. Electricity had to be home produced from generators until 1969, because of the difficulty of laying current-carrying cables across the sea bed.

Apart from visitors to the observatory and youth hostel and local craft-work, the mainstay of the island lay in its Irishness. Language and customs had survived better here than almost anywhere else and in later years a Language and Irish Heritage College was established here.

Part of the lost heritage is the old lighthouse station near the island's south eastern flank and now the haunt of choughs. It is over four hundred feet above sea level and was often obscured by fog. In the nineteenth century the old stone and slate tower was replaced by the existing round tower, but the final solution was to build another on Fastnet Rock, closer to the level of the shipping it served.

That ninety one foot high cast iron tower was commenced in 1848 and completed four years later. Subsequently the tower had a three ton rock hurled at it by Atlantic rollers and was deemed likely to collapse in 1891. The present tower, started eight years later, was built of four ton slabs of granite shipped from Cornwall. Light beam intensity had increased from 38,000 candle power in 1852 to 1,300,000 candle power in the 1960s, but today's shipping is more dependent on radar than lights.

Peter conducted a profitable sea watch in pouring rain during the evening, recording great skuas, pomarine skua and arctic skua. The first is much the commonest here, building up to as many as sixty birds in the first half of April and the first half of September. All were presumably on passage to their northern nesting grounds.

32. Great Skuas

He also spotted a sooty shearwater, a rarity in spring and not much more likely to pass by in autumn. I had sailed through flocks of thousands of these dusky birds around Stewart Island off Southern New Zealand a few years before, but have never seen one in the northern hemisphere.

Manx shearwaters are spotted out at sea off Clear during the summer, particularly during July, August and September when there are young birds to be fed, but these nest on islands further north, off County Kerry. I sometime heard their cockadoodle calls at night as they passed overhead, but there was no evidence that any actually nested on Clear Island, as they do on the Skelligs.

It seems strange that Peter had seen so much through the downpour, but it transpires that the birds fly closer inshore during foul weather, seeking protection, perhaps, but pass unnoticed, far from the shore, when fine.

My only sea bird sightings were thirty five gannets going north and a few razorbills and shags. Cape Clear is an island for people rather than sea birds but is large enough and with enough scrubby vegetation to be an ideal gathering ground for land birds commuting to far off places. The sparse bushes attract few passerines to stay all season but are a boon to weary travellers needing rest and enough sustenance for the next leg of their journey.

On my last evening a group of us went to Paddy Burke's 'watering hole' with the bank manager for a farewell drink. There was a great round of farewells, including a very warm one from Paddy's mother who emerged from the back parlour as we left. Shaking me heartily by the hand she said how much she had enjoyed knowing me, although we hadn't met until that minute! Short but sweet.

Paddy had been nine years in the merchant navy and had seen much of the world. We reminisced about Lagos, with its mangroves, coconuts and oil palms, and he plied us with tales from many other parts. This was an incongruous community, full of men who knew many of the world's far flung ports, but had not necessarily ever been to Dublin, and women who had never had the opportunity to go anywhere except the immediate bit of the mainland. Maybe the men had good reason to do most of the talking.

He was still young and un married, as was his lively sister, who was running a little business, providing meals and a 'home' for wandering seamen who came in on the fishing boats for the weekend. Some were bachelors from Cape Clear, others were drawn from other islands, serving under a Cape Clear skipper. She was one of very few unattached young women on the island, the male lament being "No young galls here that a fella could fall fer. Those above the crucial age are too broad, buxom, freckled and weathered, those below too retiring and stodgy." This, with the exception of the Burke lass, who was her own woman, possibly sussing out the field among her clients.

Peter had planned to come ashore with me next morning and enjoy two days touring the South-west, kipping down on the back seat of the car in my sleeping bag and eating out of the picnic box to save money. The long drawn out bus strike was still in progress and I was to bring him back to Skibbereen, from where he could hitch a lift.

In the event, we woke to deluging rain and he changed his mind. We made the crossing on the mail boat, the islanders going below. Ham, the German youth hosteller and I squatted on deck in the shelter of the wheelhouse out of the draught.

Ham set off on his motor scooter to Cork to catch a train for Dublin and I took the German and an island woman to Skibbereen. She was visiting her nine year old son in hospital and the journey was no pleasure to her as she spent most of its being car sick, head out of the window between necessary stops. Travel sickness is a particularly unfortunate malady for an islander.

The sun broke through the clouds as we parted company. Peter had made the wrong decision. Penelope (my car) turned west, across the head of Roaringwater Bay to Balledehob and Mizzen Head, she enjoying the uncluttered roads, me the fabulous scenery.

My memories of that patch of Mother Earth are of the brilliancs of the spring flowering gorse. Never have I seen gorse flowers so closely packed over entire bushes for mile upon mile, shedding their heady perfume of coconut and orange over the entire landscape.

3
The Skelligs, Co. Kerry
ISLAND MOUNTAINS

The Skelligs must qualify as the most dramatic of all wild sea fowl haunts along Britain's Atlantic fringes. Their two rugged peaks rise precipitously from the restless ocean off the deeply dissected headlands and inlets of South West Ireland. Their very name has a spiky feel to it. Two cathedral like rocks, they reach up from the sea as from underwater volcanoes - places to read about, to dream about, to hope to view from afar but scarcely to set foot upon. So thought this pair of holiday makers in their mid seventies.

It was July 1995 and I was driving round County Kerry with my Irish friend, Mairead Sutherland, who had retained her Iris brogue through fifty years of living in Wales and could pass for a native anywhere.

Studying the route as we drove through the evocative wilderness of MacGillycuddy's Reeks - what a wonderful name! - we noticed two tiny specks on the extreme western edge of the map. These were the outermost of many such, that seemed to have broken away from the mother country to set off on a turbulent crossing to America. It was worth a try.

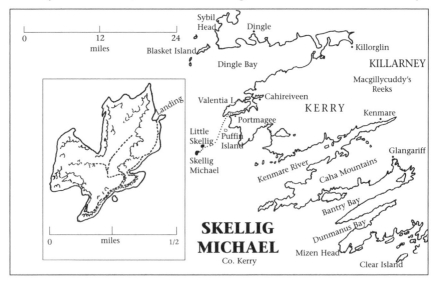

Coasting down the Ballaghisheen Pass to Waterville by Lough Curraine en route to the sandy beach at Caherdaniel, we paused at a scenic viewpoint on an arm of land reaching out to Bolus Head. That was the nearest point on the mainland to those two sea girt pinnacles on the edge of beyond.

Little Skellig lay seven miles due west of Bolus Head, Great Skellig or Skellig Michael two miles south-west of its lesser partner and eight miles from the mainland. The first rose four hundred and forty feet above the deep green Atlantic, the second seven hundred and fourteen feet - jagged peaks rearing almost vertically from the pounding waves. Only the Tearaght Rocks of the less remote Blasketts further north could approach them in majesty of form.

We needed a willing fisherman and Ballinskellig on the other side of the bay seemed a likely point of embarkation. Walking the jetty there above a jumble of fishing boats on the quiet waters in its lee, we encountered a coastguard.

"No good today. Better tomorrow. Try Portmagee."

It seemed a visit might be possible.

Portmagee had an intimate, friendly air. A row of cottages fronted the jumble of beached fishing nets and lobster pots. Boats bobbed at their moorings beyond a couple of pubs and a pierhead cafe. Two runways led down to the sea for the launching of lesser boats from vehicles.

Michael O'Sullivan, as salty and weather beaten as any, was willing to take us as part of a larger party on the morrow, with the usual proviso of "Weather permitting."

Elated, we drove over the long bridge across the Portmagee Channel to Valentia or Valencia Island and located a visitor centre. This advertised "The Skellig Experience", whatever that was - a film show, perhaps, but we were too late anyway.

The name "Valentia Island" has a familiar ring. Lying between the meteorological zones of Fastnet along the South Irish coast and Shannon along the west as far as the Aran Islands, it was a name that filtered into my sleepy consciousness, with other well known haunts such as Lundy and Fair Isle, as the early morning shipping forecast droned from my bedside radio. Gale warnings had for long been broadcast by radio telephone from Valentia when appropriate.

Another point of contact for those of us who are members of the Flatholm Society was Guglielmo Marconi who is said to have had connections with the Valentia Island Telegraph Station. ("Some Lovely Islands", Leslie Thomas, Arlington, 1982.)

That station, housed in a now defunct pitch-roofed timber hut, was transmitting messages to Newfoundland as early as 1866. These were sent along two undersea transatlantic cables laid by the ship, the "Great Eastern".

Marconi's first message to be transmitted *over* water was from Lavernock Point near Cardiff to Flatholm Island three miles offshore. This was on the 13th May, 1897. Marconi's 'cable' entering the edge of the Bristol Channel served only as an earth. His other aids were a 'radio mast' and a kite.

The connecting messages, in morse code, were truly "telegraphy without wires". A follow up was the transmission from Lavernock to Brean Down in Somerset, nine miles away across the Channel. ("Flatholm: Bristol Channel Island, Bob Jory and friends, Wincanton Press, 1995).

Returning to our farmhouse accommodation near Killorglin the lane was blocked at one point by a dappled, long-eared donkey, ruminating at right angles to the border-ing stone hedges. We drew to a halt and he turned to us with a self satisfied smile, knowing he had the upper hand.

33. Donkey

It took quite a while for Mairead to push him out of the way, one end at a time, after which he thrust his head through the driver's window to seek a reward for being so accommodating. There is something endearing and stubbornly Irish about Irish donkeys, even when they filch the apple from the hand before the first bite has been taken.

Michael O'Sullivan came to Killorglin to pick us up the next morning as part of the deal, collecting a young German couple from the lobster bar at Waterville beyond our port of embarkation. It seemed we were to be luckier than the famous Irish botanist, Robert Lloyd Praeger, chief of the National Library of Ireland from 1920 to 1924 and president of the Royal Irish Academy from 1931 to 1934. ("The Way that I went", Robert Lloyd Praeger, Allen Figgis, 1969) states:-

"The Skelligs are one of the few places in Ireland which, to my sorrow, I have not succeeded in reaching. Thrice I waited about Valentia for a good day, but the sea continued to run high and landing was declared impossible, though it was midsummer. I suppose it is salutary that some of ones desires in this world should remain unfulfilled."

It was a 'soft' morning, overcast but with little wind and no rain. We edged our way out from among boats smelling of fish and tar in Portmagee Harbour at 10.30. Valentia Island afforded shelter initially, reaching back to the old, once thriving mackerel port of Cahirsiveen at the head of the strait. The long low Atlantic swell rolling across from America met us as we peeled off from Bray Head into St. Finnan's Bay.

There were twelve passengers aboard - five Germans, five Spaniards, all young, and ourselves, and it was not the septuagenarians who were seasick!

Away on the port bow lay the hump-backed Puffin island, which accommodated Manx shearwaters, storm petrels, razorbills and guillemots as well as puffins, some of these disporting themselves on the intervening strip of sea.

The skipper slowed down as we cruised along the southern flank of Little Skellig, photographing the many thousands of resident gannets. This was very much an island for the birds. Only the most dedicated of explorers or scientists attempted to land and scramble amongst them.

34. Gannets

Like its bigger brother, Michael, this was an outlier of the Old Red Sandstone which forms the two main peninsulas between the Carboniferous limestones to the north and the Carboniferous slates to the south.

Composed of steeply dipping grits and flaggy shales, the almost vertical jointing of the rocks has been weathered to produce a splintery outline of fantastic spires and pinnacles. The strata are not red, like the Old Red Sandstone of Skokholm Island.

Their steely grey colour is lost on Little Skellig under a generous whitewashing of gannet guano, the essentially white solan geese merging into a backgound of their own making. Not that they needed any camouflage. There are no sea eagles or other potential predators this far south. The only menace was likely to be that of pillaging gulls nipping in to sneak unattended eggs. Their chosen haunt took on the character of an iceberg or giant wedding cake.

Like Grassholm in South West Wales, this gannetry is growing apace, but had had its ups and downs. A chronicler in 1700 described the birds as being "present in incredible numbers". They became scarce during the 1800s and were down to thirty pairs by 1886. No doubt they were a food source then, as for other hard living seafaring communities on St. Kilda and elsewhere. Better times for the crofters spelled better times for the gannets, with whom they shared the fish.

Bryan Nelson's 1985 map of gannet colonies in Home Waters describes Little Skellig as having more than the twenty thousand pairs reckoned to be present in 1970. Bull Rock off the next major peninsula to the south had less than a hundred pairs, and Great Saltee off South-east Ireland between a hundred and a thousand pairs at that time. ("Living with Seabirds", Bryan Nelson, Edinburgh University Press, 1986).

He reports the Great Saltee colony as having been established around 1930, about the same time as the only British mainland colony at Bempton Cliffs in Yorkshire. Both made a slow beginning, with only two or three pairs for many years before the idea took on with other gannets seeking territory and numbers shot up.

Young gannets fly off south to France, Spain or the Azores or north to the Faroes when they leave the nest, to wander the oceans before attaining breeding age. Presumably if their natal colony is overcrowded, they will look for sites elsewhere.

In Nelson's view, and he is the world's gannet authority, Little Skellig ranks among the world's five largest colonies of North Atlantic gannets anywhere. Well ahead of the rest is St. Kilda, and I have had the pleasure of viewing that spectacle too, albeit from the deck of a steamer as the captain sounded the ship's siren to put the mob of birds up from their nests when we sailed close beneath the great cliffs. The other three big colonies are Ailsa Craig and Bass Rock in Scotland, the one sailed past and the other landed upon, and Grassholm, one of my early research locations.

A BBC TV programme of 22nd May, 2005 stated there to be fifty eight thousand gannets breeding on Little Skellig in the new millennium, although some had moved to Great Saltee. Competent fishers in their own right, the gannets nevertheless were said to cash in on the by-catch thrown overboard by fishermen. The offshore waters are enriched by the Gulf Stream, which carries nutrients as well as swells into the Irish Sea, so there is enough for both.

Wherever it comes in the hierarchy of world gannetries, the solan geese clinging to the near vertical flanks of Little Skellig, like kittiwakes, are an awe inspiring sight. Once witnessed, the spectacle remains always in the memory.

Many of the vertical rocks below the main concentrations of gannets were plastered with yellow-green algae, possibly Prasiola, a lover of the excess of nitrates and phosphates that only colonial sea-birds can provide in such plenty.

There is little room for grass or herbs to provide nesting material, only three of the eight plant species recorded likely to be of any significance - these scurvy grass (a cress), sea beet and scentless mayweed. Shoreline algae form the main fabric of the nests, mostly bladder wrack and egg wrack from the upper littoral zone, plus a modicum of old rope and other debris from the flotsam. Birds were flying in with olive-brown strands dangling from their beaks to add to their menage, while others flapped across the boat to dive helter skelter into the sea after fish.

Good King Henry *(Chenopodium bonus-henricus)* was once so abundant on the Little Skellig that its local name was Skellig spinach. Leaves of sea beet can also be eaten as spinach and no doubt were by the hungry monks on the neighbouring island.

Gannets do not have the rock all to themselves. Fulmar petrels, our only northern representatives of the albatross family, and some one thousand one hundred kittiwake gulls, merge into the whitened spectacle, indistinguisable from the sea unless it is calm enough to focus binoculars.

Guillemots are present, two per cent of them bridled, wearing white pencilling around the eyes. This is a feature which increases northwards as we move into Scotland. North can also imply west, into the same degree of wind and rain, as with the substitution of carrion crows with hooded crows in Scotland and Ireland. Locally guillemots are more abundant on Douglas Head opposite the north east of Valentia Island, where there are three thousand pairs.

A few razorbills find nesting crevices around the jostling gannets, but there are more on Skellig Micheal, which is gannet free. Turf is almost non-existent for burrowing, so puffins are few, and the little stormy petrels, known to be present, are visible only at night.

As Little Skellig dropped astern, we kept a lookout for sea mammals. Porpoises and a few species of dolphins are seen in these waters, along with small schools of killer whales and the occasional minke or fin whale.

We were unlucky with those, but spotted a few Atlantic seals. These fish the sea hereabouts, but do not go ashore to drop their pups, there being no suitable beaches or caves.

We sailed through a vast but widely scattered flock of shearwaters, rafting on the surface and diving for krill and small fish. Here, too, were the delightful little tysties or black guillemots - not uncommon in Ireland and Scotland, but only just beginning to colonise Wales, in Anglesey in the north. Their crimson legs and oval white wing patches on their velvet-black, pear-shaped bodies were fashioned for underwater transit rather than flight and they stayed close above the waves.

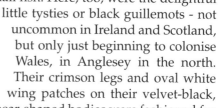
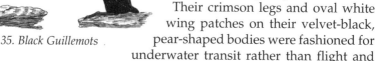

35. Black Guillemots

Skellig Michael, that fairytale castle in the sea, loomed steadily closer. Blind Man's Cove, the landing place, was in the north-east, not surprisingly in view of the potential ferocity of the prevailing south-westerlies with their so much longer 'fetch'.

Our craft drew in beside a small concrete quay constructed in 1826 a few years after the Corporation for conserving and improving the Port of Dublin" bought the island from a Waterville farmer for five hundred pounds. The land had little to commend itself to a farmer and this seemed a fair exchange from his point of view, unless he had designs on the puffins for Sunday lunches. Puffins were a traditional food on Cardigan Ireland off West Wales, eaten fresh, pickled or preserved with spices. The fifteenth century church classified puffins as fish, so they could be consumed with a clear conscience on feast days and fridays.

Each swell rolling smoothly beneath our keel lifted us gently the five feet to the top of the quay, so stepping successfully off the gunwhale onto terra firma was merely a matter of timing. Once ashore we gazed in awe at the near vertical cliffs around the cove where the Augustinian monks of old had boarded the island to scrabble up the face before the landing had been fashioned or the little roadway hacked from the rock behind.

We seemed to be at the bottom of a dark funnel, its walls flecked with green and white. The unfamiliar, long drawn out whistle of the tysties came wafting in from the sea. Most insistent, however, were the cries of kittiwakes, calling their names as they circled above our heads or perched scattered over the rock walls wherever an irregularity of the strata was sufficient to hold the deep saucer of their guano-saturated nest.

Some contained fluffy, newly hatched balls of silver-grey down, these usually in pairs. Many chicks were more advanced, near to fledging. They wore black collars and were almost ready to leave the precarious homes, from which they had been unable to stray a single step, with nowhere to place their coal-black feet.

36. *Kittiwake adult and young*

Many were restless with the urge to leave, reaching up to exercise the pale wings, each marked with a conspicuous black V, the two merging as a W when viewed from behind. Their distinctive pattern when they finally took wing, differed markedly from that of the silvery adults, whose only black is on the wing tips. Their black bills contrasted with the yellow bills of the parents, but both had gentle dark eyes, not the acid lemon of the more unruly larger gulls nor the ice blue of the gannets.

Torpedo shaped fulmars sped silently past the calling cloud of lesser birds, these alternately gliding and flapping as they exploited the air currents bellying up the cliff face. They reserved their vocal emissions for domestic sessions on the nest, where members of a pair would chat and churr companionably as they observed the passing scene.

Gradients were fairly easy as we followed along the coast to the south and we found time to look at plants as well as birds. Scentless or sea mayweed and a small-flowered version of rock spurrey snuggled up to the nesting birds, while common sorrel and sea beet occupied pockets where soil had managed to collect. Hastate orache and buck's horn plantain were as adept at clinging to rock faces as were the starry pink flowers of English stonecrop - ill named, as being more generally distributed in the rockier terrain of the North and West than in England.

At Cross Cove, another inlet opening to the north-east, the track had been roofed over, Alpine style, to deflect debris falling from the slopes above, where steepness was aggravated by the burrowing of puffins and shearwaters, There were said to be rabbits here, too, but we saw none and there were certainly no signs of their nibbling among the exuberant swards of sea campion which dominated the whole slope where the bones of the bare rock were not uppermost.

The all too familiar mat of dwarf grass and rosette plants was nowhere apparent, Red fescue grass grew in great tufts and leaves of the scurvy grass were big fleshy discs which surely would have tempted any hungry bunnies. I even spotted some of the big succulent form of buck's horn plantain *(Plantago coronopus var. maritima or ceratophyllum)* that is so closely tied to areas rich in guano but is a delicacy for any herbivore having the good fortune to come across it.

A coastal walk followed on round the lower flank of the island to serve first the lower lighthouse on the southernmost point and then zig zag up to the further one in the west below an ancient burial ground.

The serious part of the ascent to the monkish settlement started between Cross Cove and Blue Man's Rock offshore, doubling back on itself as necessary to ease the gradient. There were said to be six hundred unrelenting steps still to be scaled. We leaned into the slope and changed into a lower gear, but seemed to be functioning on auto pilot long before we reached our goal.

One of our pauses to regain breath was by an upstanding, salt-crusted monument, half Celtic Cross and half statue. This was a natural, wind-sculpted phenomenon going by the name of the Wailing Woman or the Cross of the Wailing Women, the wailing achieved by the keen wind which harried it.

Steps were narrow and steep. It was a case of "knees up Mother Brown". Some were so narrow that we could place our hands on those ahead as though scaling a ladder. This was no place for any who suffered from vertigo. Rocky edges were sometimes splintered: surfaces could be wet and slippery with a scum of algae. The wind beat upon us unrelentingly, bypassing rocks to come at us from unexpected angles.

High stepping into the dizzy gulch known as Christ's Saddle, we decided it was lunchtime and sank gratefully onto the rocks to eat our sandwiches. A lone herring gull came to join us and we had leisure to observe the myriad puffins that dotted the slopes, their burrows likely to be tortuous and shallow in such terrain.

They seemed to be everywhere, toddling back and forth in a fragrant spread of flowering sea campion as dense as that in which others of their kind nest on some of Northumberland's Farne Islands. Bouncing lightly over the rocky impedimenta like rubber balls on short orange legs, they would gaze at us quizzically. It was easy to read an expression of bewilderment on their clownish faces as they wondered why we were making such heavy weather of the ascent. Some plopped down with fish dangling untidily from their outsize, multicoloured beaks like a silvered moustache, so some of the chicks must have hatched in the dark recesses below ground.

P.G.H.Evans has carried out extensive surveys of the flora and fauna here (see "The Skelligs", by Tim O'Shea - a booklet containing reference to neither date nor publisher.) He suggests that much of the rock was formerly clad in thrift or sea pink, as in so many other western puffinries.

On Skellig, as on Grassholm, which the puffins were forced to desert when the fabric of their homes collapsed, ridges of moribund thrift had formerly separated occupied burrows. Here that surface was colonised by rock spurrey and pearlwort. On Grassholm it remained bare until the area was engulfed by the expanding gannet colony.

The hemispherical cushions adopted by thrift in such habitats lend themselves admirably to the digging of burrows into their flanks. Old plants can be very deep-rooted, if there are crevices or soil in which to root, but excessive tunnelling can undermine and destabilise them. Such effects were masked here by the advancing tide of sea campion.

Of the other burrow dwelling birds Skellig Michael is believed to support ten thousand nesting pairs of storm petrels and five thousand pairs of shearwaters. Both burrow into thrift tussocks but nest also in stable scree, old walls, and among the clitter in the monastic enclosure.

37. Storm Petrels

Puffins have been estimated at about six thousand pairs, razorbills at seven hundred and fifty pairs and fulmars at nearly a thousand pairs. As shorebirds and garbage gatherers, gulls are not as numerous as on inshore islands. There are thought to be about a hundred and twenty pairs of herring gulls, less than half this number of lesser black-backs and just the odd few greater black-backs.

The only resident land birds recorded are a few rock pipits and wheatears and a pair of choughs, but migrants take refuge here on spring and autumn passage and a few thrushes and finches have been known to overwinter.

House mice live in the lighthouse outbuildings and are said to wax larger than those of the mainland - like other small rodents islanded for long years in isolation from their forbears

Scientists have found thirteen species of molluscs - nine of snails and four of slugs. As so often with organisms unable to travel by sea, this

poses the question of how they arrived. Unlikely to have been introduced to help sustain even half starved monks, did they creep in unnoticed in lighthouse stores? This we shall never know.

An owl beetle *(Trox scaber)* was discovered here by a lighthouse keeper, far from any owl's nest where it might have gained a living in the traditional manner. As a scavenger it apparently feeds on old bones and drying skins of dead birds.

38. Owl Beetle

38a. Garden Spider

Another invertebrate present is a giant spider *(Drassodes lapidosus),* a predator reaching nearly an inch long on Skellig, this considerably more than individuals of its kind on the mainland. Its body colour is fawn tinged with pink (see "The Skelligs" by Tim O'Shea.)

As we lunched a lissom young man came jauntily down the stairway. We asked if there was much further to go.

"Not far" said he blithely. "You're almost there, more than half way."

In fact the windy gap of Christ's Saddle lies four hundred and twenty two feet up. The first of the beehive huts is at five hundred and forty five feet. The seven hundred feet of the island itself is thrust up from water ninety fathoms deep on the ocean chart - another five hundred and forty feet. He was right. We had but a fraction of the whole to go. We rose and pressed on, determined to make it to the top through the labyrinth of petrified rock profiles.

Along one stretch there was open space on both sides, the land falling away to the murmuring sea far below. It was exposed enough on this summer day. Our sympathies went out to the monks who had crouched there through wind and rain to chip a way to the spot chosen for their future life of penance.

Finally the ground levelled out and we found ourselves within the curtain wall or cashel enclosing the ancient structures. Surveyors had estimated that the enclosure occupies around a hundred by thirty yards, the buildings a hundred and fifty by fifty feet. They also reckon the island to occupy forty four acres. Does this mean horizontally, as on the map, or almost vertically, as on the ground, where it must be almost twice as large?

39. Beehive cells, medieval chapel ruins, and distant Little Skellig

We stepped first into the remains of a medieval chapel, itself in ruins. The half dozen more ancient beehive huts stretching in line beyond were more sturdily built, although without mortar, like the enclosing cashel.

Their walls were five feet thick, rising to about six feet before the gradual inward corbelling of the flattened stones began to fashion the dome of the roof. Floors were of dark, trodden earth and not necessarily flat. Each entrance was small, windows absent and interiors seemed excessively dark compared with the great vault of the sky outside. Storm petrels were the only inhabitants now and that was the way they liked it.

Stones projecting at intervals from the outside walls suggested that they may have held sods of turf packed between them to supply extra insulation - a ploy used by sealers exploiting the seals and penguins on MacQuarie Island in the great Southern Ocean (see Sub-Antarctic Sanctuary", Gillham, Gollancz, 1967.)

Perched high in the sky as we were, I was intrigued by the amount of water that seeped from many sources and trickled down between the man-made artefacts. The near vertical jointing of the rock layers might have afforded passage for mainland water passing through rock layers under the sea to seep upwards, as on many another offshore island. It might equally well have allowed rain falling in situ to seep down to an underground reservoir which released it in amounts sufficient to sustain a viable human community. Whichever way, this was the factor that had allowed the island to be colonised in the first place.

The earliest historical record of man was in 490 AD when a fugitive king took refuge here while fleeing from the king of West Munster. Like any other fugitive, he would have had to take his chance for drinking water.

The religious Anchorite community that first took up residence with Fionan on the rock in the sixth century were Celts, and they came to take rain for granted. Norsemen raided in 812 and 823 AD and they too, from lands of melting snow and glaciers, would not have been suprised to find sufficient fresh water for their needs.

It may have been different for the continental Augustinians, who settled here around 1225. Like those early Irish monks who had their origins in the desert countries of Egypt, Libya and by the Red Sea, they venerated water and must have been delighted with the clear springs oozing from rocks so high above the sea with little apparent catchment.

Wells became places of christian pilgrimage and Skellig was not only a place of pilgrimage but the most famous penitential station of all. The tests of character were severe. Pilgrims were expected to go far beyond the springs and the huts and scale hazards such as the Needle's Eye, the Stone of Pain, the Eagle's Nest and the Spindle or Spit with sheer drops to the sea, then on to straddle a fifteen foot long ridge to a tablet at the end - and get themselves back!

Most of the stone support work and walls around the monastery and possibly the three stone stairways were thought to have been constructed during the Augustinian occupation. Some walls were in ruins, as was much of the medieval chapel of St. Michael, its stones fixed with mortar and its timber and slate roof long since collapsed. The one gable wall still standing is pierced by a romanesque window which frames a fine view of the Little Skellig.

The much older beehive huts still held their own against the onslaught of centuries of foul weather. They were currently getting a little help from a team of conservationists renovating some of the furthermost. As we gazed our fill of the ancient scene the modern world impinged in a cataract of noise as a helicopter roared in to a helipad just beyond the settlement with a load of building material and other supplies. (Modern monks would have had it a lot easier.)

40. The Priest's Stone

An outstanding feature was the Priest's Stone, rising from the Monks' Graveyard behind St.Michael's Chapel, with sea campion surging around its base.

Charles Smith in "The Antient and Present State of County Kerry", 1756 states:-

"In the spring and beginning of summer the country people resort hither in small boats when the sea is calm and catch these birds" (the puffins). "They eat the flesh, which is fishy and rank, but the principal profit is made by the feathers. The birds are exceeding fat and the people who take them carry on a kind of traffic with them by exchanging two salted puffins for a peck of meal. They eat them in lent and on their fast days as well as fish."

Did they pickle their puffins in barrels of brine, I wonder, as the half cast Aboriginals with whom I worked on the Bass Strait Islands were doing still with their annual shearwater harvest at the end of the twentieth century? (See "Island Hopping in Tasmania's Roaring Forties", Gillham, Stockwell, 2000).

The lighthouses and their approach roads were built between 1820 and 1826, the workers sheltering and keeping their stores in the weatherworthy beehive huts. The southern, still functional one, is a hundred and seventy five feet above the sea, the western one, declared redundant since 1870, is three hundred and twenty seven feet up. Perhaps, like Lundy's original lighthouse, that one was set too high and often lost in sea mists or low cloud.

A new optic replaced the original oil lamp in 1909 and the beam was changed from fixed to three flashes every ten seconds. Further modernisation and conversion to electricity, generated on the spot, occurred in 1967, using the 1909 lens. The three kilowatt, hundred volt electric light has a candle power of one million three hundred thousand and can be seen for twenty seven sea miles when the weather is clear. Helicopter servicing took over from the lighthouse relief boat in 1969.

A minor ecological impact of the lighthouse keepers was the introduction of a cow, a goat a pen of poultry and possibly also the rabbits. The ferrets brought in later to rid the island of the last did not survive, but the rabbits seemed to have created little damage from what we were able to observe on our short visit.

By the time we had seen our fill almost all the other visitors had left and we hastened to do likewise. As so often, going down was harder than coming up, and certainly more scary, as we headed out into the open void instead of towards the comfort of the solid land. While there were no stretches where we had to descend backwards, as on a ship's ladder, there were plenty where we edged down sideways, with a steadying hand hovering not too far above the steps piling up behind.

I lost precious time exploring a dead end path that looked like a short cut, but we made it to the boat on time. It was just as well that I doubled back. Apparently a German woman had lost her life on that false trail a few months before. We were not sorry to be seated once more in the boat and our good skipper came up trumps with a brew of tea from the galley.

It had been well worth the physical effort. A memory to be treasured. We felt as George Bernard Shaw did, as expressed in a letter which he wrote in 1910 to a Mr. Jackson after he had visited.

"An incredible, impossible, mad place... I tell you the place does not belong to any world that you or I have lived and worked in. It is part of our dream world... The magic that takes you out, far out of this time and this world. There is Skellig Michael, ten miles off the Kerry coast, shooting straight up seven hundred feet sheer out of the Atlantic."

The really unbelievable part is that such a place should have been settled by six and seventh century monks who, for a hundred years, represented the western bastion of christianity and, indeed, of western civilisation itself, perched on its unwelcoming flanks.

4
Garinish Island, Co. Cork
AN ISLAND GARDEN

There could be no greater contrast of natural assets than between the Skelligs and Illnacullin, commonly known as Garinish Island, although they lie only forty miles apart as the crow flies over the mountains or forty eight as the cormorant flies over coastal waters.

Illnacullin, or the Island of Holly, guards the entrance to Glengarriff Harbour at the head of the twenty mile long inlet of Bantry Bay in County Cork. Protected by the Caha Mountains backing the town, it is one of a cluster of verdant islands separated by placid, salty seaways.

41. Holly

Its rocks are clothed in burgeoning vegetation caressed by soft Irish rain (73 inches per annum or 1850 mm) and cherished by horticulturalists. Conformation of the mainland deflects damaging gales and the surrounding waters are warmed by the Gulf Stream so that trees, so scarce on much of this wild Atlantic coast, are in their element.

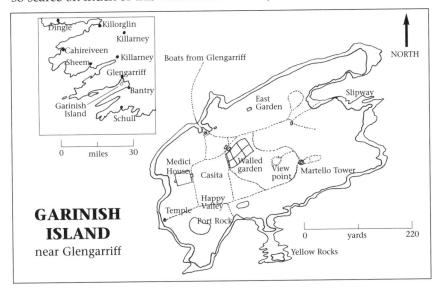

79

Glengarriff, the south facing "Craggy Glen", has been a popular tourist resort since early Victorian times The evocative description in "The Official Guide to Cork, 1960" still rings true:

"A deep secluded valley encompassed by lofty mountains whose singularly irregular and majestic outlines form the visual barriers for every part of the glen. Rocks and boulders are flung together in strange, tumultuous confusion, yet the impression is not one of roughness, for all around is a mass of luxuriant foliage, venerable oaks, elms and stately pines of the wooded glades."

The thirty seven acres (fifteen hectares) of Garinish Island in this enchanted setting, seemed the ideal place in which to create a garden and Annan Bryce, who purchased it in 1910 from the British Government, set about doing just that. The site where he and his family laboured, landscaping and planting, passed to the state on the death of his son in 1953 and is maintained as a popular destination for boat trips, the landing fees helping towards running costs. It is managed by the National Parks and Monuments Service of the Office of Public Works.

The basic geology is fundamentally similar to that of the Skelligs, this being part of the same block of Devonian Old Red Sandstone - where it borders on the Carboniferous Limestone Shales to the south, but ice action has had an ameliorating effect on the bare bones of the land here.

The Caha Mountains of the peninsula to the north occupy an upward fold or anticline in the Devonian rocks. The adjacent younger shales to the south occupy the downward fold of the bordering syncline and form the floor of Bantry Bay. This basic pattern has been accentuated by subsequent flooding of the long inlet to form a ria or drowned valley.

Moving glaciers produced a swarm of drumlins - piles of morainic, ice-transported material - centred around Bantry town at the head of the bay opposite Glengarriff. These were subsequently moulded by the lower layers of the Cork:Kerry ice sheet, which was deflected by the synclinal valley after crossing the Caha Mountains, so that most of the drumlins became aligned along the inlets.

Many were left as islands, while the fertile, ice-transported soils on the mainland lent themselves to agriculture and arboriculture - the fresh green of their pastures and spinneys less formidable than the dark gorse, heather and bogland of the backing mountains. What more idyllic place in which to create a garden than one of these sequestered offshore gems?

Like that other ria of Milford Haven across the Irish Sea, this twenty miles of deep water is used by big oil tankers coming in to discharge their crude oil at Whiddy Island, which is on the Bantry side of the inlet and has little effect on the idyllic scenery of the Glengarriff side.

Bear Island, nearer the mouth of the ria, was formerly a British naval base but has lapsed into disuse. Beyond this, towards Dursey Island are the abandoned workings of a lode of copper slicing through the Old Red Sandstone, along with the ruined dwellings of the miners in the so-called "Cornish Village". The benign fertility of the plankton rich waters nurture a shellfish farm.

Despite the industrial enterprises, past and present, Thackeray's words still ring as true as when he wrote them in 1843.

"Around the pretty inn of Glengarriff Harbour there is a country of the magnificence of which no pen can give an idea. Were such a bay lying upon English shores, it would be a world's wonder. Perhaps if it were on the Mediterranean or the Baltic English travellers would flock to it in hundreds." ("Irish Sketch Book", William Makepeace Thackeray, 1843.).

For the sheer richness of animal life, the voyage to the island in 1995 proved more rewarding than our spell ashore. The aquatic mammals distributed throughout were common or harbour seals, not the long-nosed, grey Atlantic seals that we are used to seeing along the Welsh coast. Both species are present around Ireland, the harbour seals favouring the sandy bays and patchy saltings at the head of inlets such as these, the greys choosing more turbulent waters off headlands and the outer isles.

In fact the many groups of seals that we watched had not pulled out on sand bars or gravel banks exposed as the tide fell but on rocky knolls coated with upshore wracks and lichens. They exuded the same ambience of luxurious idleness as the grey seals which feature more typically in such rocky situations. It is odd that creatures so much more at home under water should so enjoy sunbathing when opportunity allows.

42. Harbour Seals

Our little craft curved in towards the clusters of reclining seal flesh, some sleek and dark, like giant slugs, as freshly heaved out of the limpid water. Others were paler, plain or speckled, and the colour of Irish soda bread rolls, as the pelt dried and the fur fluffed out.

Their heads were rounder and their faces flatter than those of their Atlantic counterparts. Snub noses and big dreamy brown eyes gave them a pixyish appearance. 'Pretty' was a suitable adjective and one that was certainly not applicable to the Atlantic greys, with their long pointy muzzles and noses sloping blandly down from the forehead. They were as Jersey cows are to more angular Friesians, or dish-faced small white pigs to large, 'pretty' not so apt in this instance.

Regarding us curiously, they would lift one end or the other from the wet rocks to let in whiffs of warm, drying air. Adults were smaller than adult greys and youngsters larger than their grey contemporaries, being born at a later stage of development. As our visit was at the height of their midsummer breeding season, there were some of each.

Here were none of the doe-eyed, furry white pups that lie prone in our Welsh coves for three weeks after being dropped by their dams, usually between September and November. Harbour seal pups shed their baby fur at or just after birth, appearing sleek and waterproof right from the start.

This fits them for birth on tidal sand banks such as those of East Anglia where they are a popular tourist draw. Those babes will be washed off at the return of the first tide. Atlantic pups are deposited well above high water mark by wise mothers and can sleep high and dry in their polar bear overcoats until these moult and the milk supply is cut off. They can live on the fat imbibed with the rich creamy milk for a while, but hunger eventually drives them out to sea, where they learn to feed themselves on molluscs, crustaceans and cephalopods until they develop a technique for catching the more elusive fish that will form their staple diet in the years to come.

Glengarriff Harbour pups have the option of remaining ashore for longer, by lolloping higher up the rocks as the tide advances, but would be unwise to do so, as their dams suckle them at sea as well as on land. The sooner they get used to life in the water the more adept they will be when left to their own devices.

We were lucky to be here during the pupping season, because it is only then that members of this species gather in such large groups, being more solitary than the greys at other seasons. They were hauled out on smooth, mounded rocks, about a dozen together. Judging from the widths of the bands of different growths, tidal range was small in these enclosed waters. The favoured knolls rose from the limpet:barnacle zone through narrow belts of spiral and channelled wracks and bristly black Lichina, a marine lichen, to smoother covers of black, grey and orange lichens in the splash zone.

Matching rock shelves occurred at this level on mainland shores, but these often rose steeply into heather or gorse and to within reach of possible predators, at gradients which would have defeated even more mobile sea lions. Pliant birches, upstart sallows and red-trunked Scots pines gave shade and shelter to the upper littoral zone.

Drifting the last lap of the voyage through this summery paradise, where exotic trees and shrubs had been moulded deftly into folds of the landscape among residual wildlings, we were mindful of Lloyd Praeger's interpretation of the site:

"A fairy like, island studded bay, facing full south, very sheltered, almost frostless in winter and seldom too hot in summer - though the midges may be pesky".

We stepped ashore on the north coast, the scene enhanced by 'living fossil' conifers from the Far East and the Far West. Spreading lacy arms towards us was a dawn redwood *(Metasequoia leptostroboides)* from the heart of China and a bald or swamp cypress *(Taxodium distichum)* from the Florida Everglades. This leviathan when grown can overcome aeration problems in soil permeated by stagnant water, by elevating pointy knee roots in the fresh air, mangrove fashion.

Such arboreal gems are more often encountered in arboreta in the southern counties of England, but they are not averse to living in the windy West at higher latitudes than were tolerated by their ancestors. Gardens on our Atlantic fringes such as these occur not only on Trescoe in the Scillies but at Inverewe in the Western Highlands of Scotland, where frosts are notably rarer than at an equivalent number of degrees north on the less favoured American side of the great ocean. Inverewe may experience no more than two degrees of frost in some years, this due to the benign influence of the Gulf Stream or North Atlantic Drift.

The rather yew-like annual shoots of fresh green leaves, which are shed at the end of summer, complete with the twiglets which bear them, are similar in the two species.

The trick for telling them apart is that those of the dawn redwood grow in opposite pairs and those of the swamp cypress alternately. Splashes of continuous colour were supplied by Rhododendrons and Azaleas. Glossy-leaved Camellias were equally at home on the acid substrate, their pink and white flowers so neatly symmetrical as to appear machine-made when they fell, intact, to embellish the paths.

The strawberry trees *(Arbutus unedo)*, bearing clusters of little white bell flowers and strawberry-like fruits simultaneously, might be indige-

43. Strawberry Tree

nous here. We are more used to seeing them in gardens but they are native in Western Ireland, in Cork and Kerry in the South and Sligo in the North.

Whether spontaneous or planted, they were moulded skilfully into the whole and such verdure does not appear overnight. In the early part of the nineteenth century Garinish was a military outpost and such little soil as remained was a thin acid peat, best suited to the native gorse and heather. When Annan Bryce became the owner in 1910 his first tasks were to import quantities of topsoil and establish peripheral shelter belts.

He sought the services of Harold Peto, an accomplished landscape architect, and old records show that about a hundred workmen were employed during the formative stages. A range of conifers was used to deflect the salty winds, from spreading pines to pyramidal spruces, the pencil cypresses saved for more tender, Mediterranean style tableaux within their mild embrace.

New paths were made, curving round rocky obstacles, and flights of steps constructed to deal with steeper gradients. Ornamental buildings were erected in key positions, along with stone walls and clipped hedges.

The horticulturalist responsible for development and maintenance in later years was Murdo MacKenzie, who continued to adapt his plantings to contours and soils. One particularly striking combination was the sea of scarlet tulips beneath a profusion of tulip-shaped Magnolia flowers bursting from overarching branches.

Elusive sunshine cast warming rays over paths leading between forget-me-not blue borders and what appeared to be neatly trimmed mounds of lavender. The walled garden with its neatly clipped shrubs and shapely dwarf conifers was particularly fine, although the herbaceous borders would be coming into their full glory later in the season. Pink roses, mauve Wistaria and summer jasmin climbed the walls among a profusion of hybrid Clematis plants and the powder blue bobble flowers of Ceonothus bushes.

The focal point of the ensemble is the Italian Garden, the brain child of Peto. This is constructed around a rectangular water lily pool, the central feature an athletic figure fashioned apparently in bronze. Container plants, including bonsais, graced the surrounding paving, while a pair of stone lions guarded the steps down from the pillared viewing point. Classical style buildings at either end were swathed in flowers. One is the

Casita, the other the Medici House. Pillars framed superb views across the translucent waters of the bay to the looming shapes of the Caha Mountains in one direction and a wide sweep of neatly manicured lawn in another.

Whiffs of myrtle with aromatic leaves and fragrant white flowers permeated the air, while sophisticated versions of the deciduous Fuchsias, which thrive so prolifically in the mainland hedges throughout the South, were hung with crimson and purple bells

From here it was a short step to the Grecian temple a little further along this same west coast and commanding similarly striking views of Bantry Bay and the mountains. Terrain close at hand, with plants nestling among mounded rocks and water lapping in little coves, added greatly to the enjoyment of

44. *View from the Italian Garden south-west across Bantry Bay.*

the whole - the natural landscape providing an intriguing backdrop for the horticulturalists' art. Pines wearing green socks of damp moss were etched against water of an intense steely blue.

Back down the staircase constructed from the local blue limestone shales, we were walking between avenues of Italian cypresses. Happy Valley was an intriguing mixture of trees and chunky outcrops shaggy with lichens, these lowly plants witness to the absence of atmospheric pollution seeping across from the oil tankers moored on Whiddy Island.

Particularly striking hereabouts was *Embothrium coccinium* from South America, its long spikes of showy red flowers giving it the popular name of Chilean fire bush. The only member of its genus hardy enough to survive in our region, it bears its brilliant flowers in terminal or axillary racemes. In sharp contrast was the flowering dogwood, with conspicuous white bracts surroundung clusters of small dark flowers.

We followed a side path to a south facing cove, one arm of which straggled seaward to form the tidal island of Yellow Rock. Seals nearby were drowsing the afternoon away. This was a place to come to spot waders on passage. Today we saw only the odd cormorant and oyster catcher.

Back inland, with a pool to the right and the 'jungle' to the left, we ascended more steps to the island summit, surmounted by the Martello Tower - a substantial time-mellowed relic from ancient history. Built of rugged grey stone, it crowned a massive bluff on the highest point, its support undercut on one face. Watchers from this strategic point benefited from panoramic views in all directions, but might still have had difficulty in spotting an enemy creeping up on them through the intricacy of islets and headlands. Nearby is another, more modern viewpoint.

We had time to visit the second boat slipway in a deeply indented bay to the east before returning to browse around the gardens. Tucked unobtrusively by the wayside were unassuming little plants of St. Patrick's cabbage. This was no cabbage, but a saxifrage *(Saxifraga spathularis)*, native to the south and west coastal counties of Eire, from shoreline to mountain top.

It is naturalised throughout Great Britain as a rampant garden plant, but more often as a very similar hybrid with the Pyrenean saxigrage *(Saxifraga umbrosa)*. This is what most of us know as London pride and it has been accorded an urban sounding scientific name as *Saxifraga X urbicum,* the X indicating its hybrid status.

There is a strong flavour of the Antipodes among the plants introduced to this balmy habitat. Favourites are the Leptospermums of the Eucalyptus family, white flowered, as in the wild, or more dashing pink and red flowered cultivars. The coastal tea tree *(Leptospermum laevigatum)* thriving here flourishes along the windswept, salt-rimed coasts of its homelands on the mutton bird islands of New Zealand, Tasmania and South-east Australia, where the shearwaters come swirling in after dark to their burrows intertwined among its roots.

Like its close relatives, it is an important sand binder and stabiliser of rocky slopes, battling the elements as deformed, stag-headed dwarfs or growing to sizable trees in kindlier conditions. Prolific flowerers, their copious honey flow is a boon to bees and apiarists.

There are fifty species, all but three of them Australasian, and another favourite grown in G.B. and I. is *Leptospermum scoparium.* This is the one from which Captain Cook and his crew plucked leaves to brew up for their tea. The name of tea tree or ti tree, has come to be adopted for a number of closely related species, although the local manuka is often used 'down under', and kanuka for a spinier-leaved species. An increasing number of uses have been found for tea tree oil in medicines, ointments and insect repellents.

45. Tea Tree

Another name for which Captain Cook is responsible is the New Zealand cabbage tree for

Cordyline australis, which is so popularly planted in our southern counties. The succulent leaf rosettes were eaten as cabbage by his crew, apparently they tasted similar, although the palm-like tree is even less like a cabbage than St. Patrick's.

Some of the five hundred or so Eucalyptus species are also familiar here, as is another group of this family, the bottle brushes (Callistemon spp.). Like the gums and stringy-barks, their flowers consist largely of a mass of stamens, usually red, but sometimes yellow or white.

46. Bottle Brush

It is their clustering around the stem below the terminal tuft of leaves that gives them a resemblance to a flambuoyant bottle brush.The ensuing cylinders of brown woody fruits, individually like those of tea trees, usually remain on the twigs for three years. In Nature the tiny seeds within are generally only released after a forest fire- as are those of the more substantial Banksia bottle brushes named after the Kew Gardens explorer, Sir Joseph Banks.

From the same region come the Grevilleas, a favourite at Garinish with their weirdly shaped red, yellow or orange flowers. King of this genus is the stately silky oak *(Grevillea robusta).* Mighty as an oak, it is quite unrelated, being in the Proteaceae like the Chilean fire tree. The oak simile is likely to have arisen from the beautifully figured timber rather than the deeply dissected leaves or great bunches of orange-yellow flowers.

Another Australian here is *Dacrydium franklinii,* the Huon pine of Tasmania's temperate rain forests. Not a true pine, this is a Podocarp, or member of the plum-pine family. The branches droop, the tiny leaves overlap and the little cones are fleshy.

Stepping back into the boat for the return voyage to Glengarriff, we felt we had been in another land, traces of which were by no means lacking from the fine, cliff-backed flower beds of that delightful town.

My only previous visit to Garinish Island had been earlier in the season, on 2nd May and earlier by thirty two years. Then, in 1963, the boat fare from Glengarriff was five shillings (twenty five pence in new money) and the entry fee to the gardens half a crown (two shillings and sixpence or twelve and a half new pence). We saw but a single seal on the voyage, but there were diving tysties and hovering terns, as well as shags, cormorants and oyster catchers.

Most of the flowers that we encountered in this later July were already blooming during that mild spring and were being well served by bumble bees. Others included swathes of pink Cyclamen and blue Anemones, interrupted by spiky Colletia anchor plants.

Knowing Sphagnum peat to be the main ingredient of the native soils, we expected to see the use of lime to counteract the acidity. Instead we saw great piles of compost in a "back garden plot" and a gardener spreading a thick mulch of dead, and surely toxic pine needles over the flower beds.

"We need only to add humus" said he.

The atmosphere of the Italian gardens, with their colonades, pergolas and pillars, mouldering British lion and carved Eastern figures, was captivating. There were small pools with stepping stones, and large pools floored with pennies - plus one silver sixpence from some hopeful wishing a more impossible wish. Most of the treasure trove had been there for some time, the shine replaced by verdigris. The removal of some had left green, "limpet" circles on the concrete.

47. Cyclamen

5
The Aran Islands, Co. Clare
A SEA-GIRT LIMESTONE REEF

While much of the Carboniferous Limestone of Ireland's heart is blanketed by peat, enough of the calcareous matrix surfaces to delight the springtime traveller with cowslips by the million. These delightful flowers lined the roads and wafted away across the fields in runnels and pools of yellow, although practically absent on the Burren itself, where the hybrid with primrose is not uncommon.

It was 28th May 1979 and our party of naturalists from Wales was headed towards the botanical best of all the Irish limestone where it meets the western ocean in the world famous Burren and its outliers, the Aran Islands.

Threading Galway's dockland to the Beach Hotel at Salthill, Galway Bay stretched across to the distant islands sleeping in the blue Atlantic. The perfect arc of a rainbow materialised against a backdrop of threatening nimbus, after which unblinking sunshine produced a clarity of light that remained until the golden ball finally sank below the watery horizon.

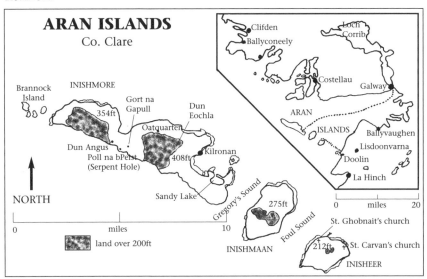

No less than a hundred and seven of those elegant sea-fishing ducks, the mergansers, had assembled offshore here in February of that year and mute swan flocks could build up to well over two hundred by July.

Our evening 'bird walk' yielded only three mergansers and twenty five mute swans, but shimmering flocks of common terns flashed silvered wings in the flattening sunrays above meandering cormorants. Oyster catchers and hooded crows foraged along the shore and the air was full of cavorting swallows and swifts.

A squally night, punctuated by torrential showers, blossomed into a brilliant day of sun and wind. We spent it exploring afoot, learning the rudiments of what we might expect on those enchanted islands that beckoned from across the sea.

A few miles to the west we followed a fringing beach which narrowed into a spit connecting the tied island of Gentian Hill to the mainland. The sward of this grassy knoll was lusher than that of the outer isles but supported many of its botanical highlights, some in greater profusion.

Built of glacial drift, the ice-smoothed pebbles were of granite as well as limestone. The hill rose ever higher, to the deeply indented seaward tip where it dropped sharply, in contrast to the tail-away in a long bar stretching out through the intertidal zone. The great curving storm beach of the approach seemed to have been driven progressively towards the partially enclosed bay separating it from the mainland, overtopping itself to spill back onto the flower-filled grassland behind.

As the layers of pebbles were lifted and rolled over the crest of the ridge, they exposed the remnants of vegetation which they had engulfed many years before. What had been a freshwater scrub of alders and reeds before burial had emerged as a tide-washed peat bed. The odd salt-rimed tree stump was surrounded by a peaty tumble of sodden branches flattened to oval cross sections by the weight of stones above.

Sea life had taken over, crabs, jellyfish, mermaid's purse egg cases and inumerable shellfish. Limestone beach boulders were pitted with tunnels, small ones excavated by marine worms *(Polydora ciliata)* and large ones by molluscan rosy-nosed rock borers *(Hiatella arctica)*, these sufficiently commodious to provide refuges for rough periwinkles.

The pebbles themselves contained the fossilised remains of other sea creatures that had lived three hundred and twenty million years ago when the rock was being laid down. Here were brachiopods or lamp shells, crinoids or sea lilies and various corals.

Fulmars and sandwich terns mingled with the oyster-catchers, common terns and four gull species, with shelducks offshore. Rock and meadow pipits graded inland to stonechats and linnets and these to more everyday birds.

It was, however, the flowers of Gentian Hill proper that won the day. Not for nothing was it named for the spring gentians *(Gentiana verna)* that were at peak of flowering, their vivid blue petals erect when we arrived but spreading as the sunlight strengthened. We associate these with the Alps, so they were far from their usual homeland, but obviously finding all they needed here, as they did also on the Aran Islands.

48. Spring Gentian

Small creatures had been nibbling at the azure perfection of some, leaving just the upstanding coronal fringe of white around their centres. Most abundant plant eaters were the burnet moth caterpillars, some already ensconced in papery yellow cocoons attached to grass stems, but these confine their feeding forays to trefoils and clovers. Was this, perhaps, the work of slugs or beetles?

A splendid Arctic-alpine present here in profusion was mountain avens *(Dryas octopetala)* on a low cliff facing sheltered waters towards the mainland. This does not occur on the Aran Islands although it is one of the much sung highlights of the Burren where it descends right to sea level, despite the low latitude.

Early purple orchids, usually more at home in woodlands, mingled with green-winged orchids and twayblades among primroses and cowslips at prime of flowering. Violets and deep blue milkwort grew with pignut and bird's foot trefoil among lush grasses and low-growing creeping willow. Twenty one species were flowering here and another twenty nine on the storm beach, among sea campion, sea radish and kidney vetch.

By six thirty next morning we were assembled on the waterfront at Galway watching young calves being swung aboard the Aran steamer. These would be auctioned on the quay after arrival at Inishmore. They were Hereford X Friesian crossbreds, likely to fetch considerably more than before Ireland's entry into the EEC in 1973.

After being weaned and reared as store cattle on the island, they would be shipped back to the richer grazing of the mainland for fattening. Stores make few demands on their owners, so are favoured by islanders who spend much of their time at sea or wish to reduce their work load with advancing years. The stock are necessarily hardy and can be fattened on grass in a few months when returned to kindlier conditions.

A primary island export - big square stacks of oarweed or Laminaria stalks tied in bundles - were ranged along the Galway quay. These are known locally as sea rods, the supporting axes remaining after severance of the pliable fronds, which are left to rot on the beach in heaps for later addition to the land as compost. The stalks dry to a woody consistency and are of no value as fertiliser.

On other islands, where there is more native soil, the sinuous, flattened oar blades, may be burned as kelp, the powdery ash yielding iodine, which is much easier to export! Aran islanders have no peat for their own essential needs, with none to spare for burning kelp, and they needed this bounty from the sea to help grow their grass and crops, so little kelp was produced. Drying lessened the weight when the rods were being manhandled onto the steamer headed for Connemara for use in the manufacture of nylon.

On arrival at Inishmore, we observed similar stacks on the quay, awaiting export. Oarweeds grow only in the lower, sub-littoral zone, so are often collected from boats, but much is washed ashore by the great gales of winter.

We trooped aboard and took up station around the ship's rail to savour the voyage to the four mile distant reef of limestone stretching out from the coast of Clare in a west-north-westerly direction. Marine erosion has broken the reef into three main parts. Inishmore is eight and a half miles long, Inishmaan and Inisheer much less. All are two to three miles wide. The highest point on Inishmore is four hundred and six feet.

As we drew away into the broad expanse of Galway Bay, terns, gulls and cormorants fell behind, to be replaced by gannets and shags. Then came the bona fide ocean goers, Manx shearwaters and the occasional swallow-sized storm petrel 'walking the waters'.

The biggest thrill was a great northern diver and another diver which we failed to identify. When the islands drew near, auks began to appear, principally razorbills and guillemots, but also a few black guillemots.

49. Great Northern Diver

Kilronan, the port and only town of Inishmore, is tucked back into Killeany Bay which opens to the east with the bulk of the island sheltering it from the worst of the weather.

There were twenty four of us, here to study the unique island flora, and tourism was not too well developed in the 1970s, so we had plenty of time to admire the informalities of Killeany Bay, with its untethered donkeys ambling around and sleeping on the sandy beach while we awaited transport.

We were to be domiciled at Oatquarter in the island centre and that was four miles away. Pony traps or jaunting cars were the normal means of island travel, but they accommodated only three at a time. Three into twenty four goes eight. Finally three went in a pony trap with the luggage and the rest, seven at a time, in the mini bus.

Accommodation was in private houses, very welcoming and wholly adequate but somewhat cramped. Some folk were put two in a double bed, three occupied a room meant for two, a lady slept in a relative's house and a gent on a bed made up in the dining room after we had finished our evening meal.

Rations were more than adequate, but 'afters' consisted inevitably of rhubarb, a fine bed of which swarmed over a pile of rotted kelp in a corner of the walled garden. This crop thrives in the cool dampness of our Atlantic fringes and is often a mainstay of Scottish island crofters. The broad leaves had an added use here, as soil makers and pliable debris to ram down into soil-swallowing rifts in the bedrock.

To move around as a party of twenty four would have been wholly out of keeping on this flowery paradise set in the western sea and we worked in smaller groups comparing notes when we joined up at each day's end.

This was a land of rock - flat limestone pavement with negligible cracks, massive sculptures of angular clints separated by plant-filled grykes and tiers of limestone terraces faced by vertical cliffs. The whole was enmeshed with a chequerboard of stone walls, the rocks loosely piled, with fresh air blowing through. Some showed erect stones at intervals with others leaning obliquely between. Some had heavy stone gateposts. All had piled stones in lieu of gates.

Cottagers who kept a house cow took their bucket or milk can and stool to extract the bounty in the field, rather than demolishing a gate twice a day to take the cow to a milking parlour. We observed one legged milking stools, obviously more practical on soft turf than the hard standing of a byre. Mostly the milk had to be shared with those for whom it was produced.

By no means all the calves were imported. A number, both would-be milkers and beefers, had just been born on the island and were frisking round the little fields when not clamped to the parental milk bar. Some nurse cows suckled two calves, not necessarily both their own. Others had three or four, so imports were needed to make up their full quota.

It was Syd Johnson, engineer, who spotted a calf's front feet protruding from under the tail of a straining cow. We backtracked to inform the farmer we had noticed digging with a long-handled spade, not turning sods over, but just stirring the soil, as with a hoe. The cow was not his. It belonged to another on the further side of the bay.

50. *Bovine birth*

An Aran farmer's land is not in compact holdings, but is shared out amicably in scattered lots so that all have some good pasture with adequate soil depth in declivities, some barren limestone and some deep sand areas behind the spreading beaches - like Hebridean crofters, each with their portion of good sandy machair land behind the beach and poor peaty blackland on the backing moor.

A man and a girl came trundling up the track driving two cows and we took them to assess the situation. They decided the mother-to-be needed help: a first calver with a steer in the same enclosure likely to take exception to the newborn. (Tom Jones of the Welsh Ministry of Agriculture and Fisheries thought otherwise - not with Mum on hand to fight her corner).

The girl tried to mount the rusty bicycle she was wheeling to zip round the bay to the owner, but Syd had to bring his expertise to bear on the machine first, replacing the chain three times before it held, enabling her to rattle off over the natural cobbles.

Jill Wisbey, passing half an hour later, reported that the calf had been born, one of the men in attendance dismantling the 'gate' and ushering the steer into the next field while the other supported the calf on its wobbly legs as it siphoned out the rich beestings or colostrum so essential to enhance its disease resistance during vulnerable infancy.

In spite of the low milk yields produced by cows on the island's frugal pastures, calves were usually weaned off milk later here than on the mainland to give them a good start, so a pleasant summer loomed ahead of this late May arrival. It might spend eighteen months here or be taken to the annual Michaelmas Fair in late September when surplus stock is sold off to buyers from Galway for fattening on mainland provender before export to England.

With only one or two milch cows per holding, these had to supply the household with milk, some for butter churning, but apparently not for cheese making. During my wartime farming years calves had to be restrained from taking more than their alloted share of the milk - a simple matter with calf pens, loose boxes and byres. I wondered how they solved this problem on Aran where the cattle were out in the fields throughout the year.

A vision of calves being lifted over stone gateways for set periods seemed a little odd, but not completely un-Irish. In fact nurse cows suckling a full quota of young calves probably did not contribute to the domestic hearh. Older calves were put in little groups in separate fields and bucket fed, to wean them gradually onto grass.

The coat color of normally black cattle had a dark brown sheen - this apparently due to copper deficiency - something we experience in South Wales on Liassic rather than Carboniferous limestone grazings.

Horses were sometimes sold at the Michaelmas fairs, even pigs, although few were reared and most of those were slaughtered to be home-cured and hung in kitchen ceilings, neighbours killing at different times and sharing the spoils that did not lend themselves to long term preservation.

Sheep and goats were kept, some producing twins. Sheep, which supply meat and wool for the famous Aran knitwear, were sometimes free range, tweaking green feed from crevices on unenclosed land where they could, some already shorn. Goats also ranged over rocky unfenced land, but were often hobbled or tethered to quell their natural exuberance. Few walls would have been proof against their athleticism. They produced hides as well as milk and presumably meat.

Donkeys ranged freely over rocks, dunes and beaches, serving their masters well as mounts or when their paired wicker panniers were laden with seaweed, potatoes or rye. Some hauled small jaunting carts with stores from the pierhead at Killeany.

Potatoes are the staple arable crop, growing well where few others will and yielding as much as 15 tonnes per hectare. They have a high food value, particularly in conjunction with home produced lard - hence British nutritionists' war against chips in the new millennium, where obesity is more of a problem than adequate subsistence.

We saw no land ploughed in long furrows by horse:mule:donkey teams or tractors, as on Cape Clear Island a decade before. Here all were planted on hand prepared sites, often shallow lazy beds standing not much more than a foot above the bald rock. On Clear Island the beds were higher to keep them above standing water in winter. Here they were low because every scrap of soil had to be hand mixed from beach sand, seaweeds and any organic waste that could be scraped together.

Indeed, even non-organic waste was brought into use. There was no municipal refuse collection. Tins, bottles, cardboard crates and no doubt modern packaging   proved vital for filling up the broader grykes between slabs. It would be foolish to lose laboriously hand made soil down crevices. Some such as rhubarb leaves were favourites as a mulch for overlying rubble but allowing longer roots to penetrate moist horizons below.

51. *Lazybeds on ribbed rock*

Lazy beds tended to be five to six feet or up to two metres wide, the soil above the rock added in layers. If there was a grass sward present before, the turf was skimmed and turned back on itself, grass side down, over a layer of seaweed. More sand and seaweed were added and any available soil used in the uppermost layer into which the seed potatoes would be placed. - in two to four rows.

Earthing up, with whatever could be scraped from the marginal trenches, was done about two months into the growing season. Weeds were removed and added to compost heaps and copper sulphate or bluestone solution sprayed on before harvest to guard against the dreaded potato blight. Planting was in March or April and lifting from July on, for storage until needed - for humans or winter cattle feed. Clamps were covered with straw and earth clods, all of which would be recycled into the next crop - if not contaminated with disease.

Other root vegetables and Brassicas were grown on a smaller scale and we noticed plenty of onions, leeks or shallots in corners of fields and gardens.

Raised beds on sandier fields behind the beaches entailed less cartage and we saw material being dug from sand pits behind a spacious northern bay. The seaweed with which it was incorporated had been stored on the sands to rot, often under tarpaulins held down with old fishing nets pegged to the sand. It was probably collected here as driftweed, because seaweed can only grow where there is underlying rock for attachment.

Nearby fields had been sown with perennial ryegrass or barley, ground barley meal an important pig fodder. The grasslands, pasture rather than meadow, bore a wealth of flowers and many were awash with bulbous buttercups and field daisies. Early purple orchids, including a fair proportion of rare white ones, were quite common among the blue of Buxbaum's speedwell and paler lamb's lettuce. Equally bright were the slightly shorter green-winged orchids, these recently lifted by taxonomists from the genus Orchis to Anacamptis - that formerly the terrain only of pyramidal orchids.

52. *Early Purple Orchid*

Rye was probably the commonest cereal, this sometimes sown on the lazy beds, rotating with the potato crop. This in itself precluded the possibility of mechanised sowing or reaping, but there was nothing mechanised about Aran farming.

Sown when the potatoes were lifted, from July on, it was used at that time principally as thatching straw, for which it was pulled rather than cut, to utilise the whole length. The tufty roots would soak up the damp during drying, leaving the butts clean for the final tidying up. A layer of rough grass was inserted between house rafters and straw, the result looking quite insubstantial and sprouting many an awned head of rye in season, where grain had been left behind to germinate on high.

Tied sheaves were not stooked in wigwams preventing plant growth beneath, but leaned against walls to dry in the sun - a worrying time when sunshine was in short supply. Rye straw to be fed to livestock was cut green with a scythe before the ears were likely to be shed. The crop was dried loose in swathes, like hay, turned occasionally and then

53. *Rye sprouting from thatch*

stacked in ricks, tied down with long straw ropes weighted with stones, like those used to hold house thatches in place.

Separating the ears from the straw and the grain from the chaff was achieved by ancient means, still in use in many Mediterranean lands at that time. Flailing was achieved by taking bunches of straw in the hands

97

and beating them against a rock to shake the heads off. Winnowing, to separate the nutritious grain from the lightweight chaff, was done in the time honoured fashion of dropping handfuls from a height when the wind was at the right strength to waft the chaff away while letting the heavier grain fall onto a handy collecting surface.

Geologists attribute the horizontal nature of successive beds of Carboniferous Limestone to their solid foundation on the underlying Galway Granites, stabilising them against subsequent folding and faulting. Strata dip so gently to the south that they appear almost level.

Scraped free of subsequent deposits by movement of the Pleistocene ice sheet, the margins of successive bedding planes may form terraces stepped one above the other, their edges manifested as cliffs up to twenty feet high, though mostly less. These deflect salty winds and protect narrow belts of scrub dominated by hazel and hawthorn, with dogwood, spindle, a little purging buckthorn and even the odd stunted oak.

Water passing along the bedding planes emerges into the open at the foot of each line of cliffs, sometime in quantities sufficient to encourage marsh plants. Osiers had been planted in some such sites, producing crops of withies. Cut close to the ground when about seven feet high or up to two metres, the stems are used for weaving baskets and donkey panniers.

Such woody growths can be regarded as the climatic climax vegetation. We were interested in tracing the early phases of the plant succession leading up to this community.

Incongruously upstanding blocks of Connemara Granite are littered around the island, adding a surreal touch to the windshorn levels. These foreign igneous rocks are erratics brought south by moving ice and dumped as this melted.

Today's few islets of acid plants must have survived from post glacial times, very likely on patches of non-limey Boulder Clay accompanying the erratics and subsequently eroded away, either by the elements or by husbandry.

Oxyphiles (acid lovers) persist only where a dark layer of organic detritus has built up on the underlying, ice-smoothed rock surface. Scottish heather or ling predominates, protecting pockets of tormentil and heath bedstraw, with bog cotton and lousewort where damper.

Horizontal slabs are smoother of texture than most granites and do not lend themselves to prolific lichen growth. Rain water settling in slight declivities brimful after recent rain, had plumped up their sparse lining of blue-green algae, some with a pinkish tinge, others green or black.

Gelatinous lichens, swollen with rain, collect fragments of debris sufficient for seeds of rosette plants to germinate. Tiny thrift and plantain clumps inhabit dents in the rocks only an inch across and are able to put forth little clusters of flowers.

Standing water, aided by lichen acids, undercuts the pool brinks, while puny trickles broaden cracks for mosses and seedlings to gain a hold. The only liverwort we saw was a dark red Frullania with dry, pitcher-shaped leaves.

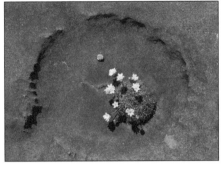

54. Early colonisation by thrift

As the hollows deepen they become colonised by ever spreading mats of Irish saxifrage *(Saxifraga rosacea)*. Formerly referred to as a variety of mossy saxifrage *(Saxifraga hypnoides var. sternbergii)*, this is now separated on its erect rather than nodding flower buds and leaves three to five lobed instead of linear or three lobed as in the other.

We gazed entranced on the mat of white flowers, closely grouped but only an inch or so high. They created a veritable rock garden - more reminiscent of the Alps or the Arctic than our own modest altitude and latitude. These cold-resistant plants benefit from South West Ireland's cool summers, just as the Lusitanean element that we met on Cape Clear Island benefits from the mild winters. Both groups enjoy the spaciousness and lack of competition from more aggressive species.

With them here on the partially bare limestone were clusters of the equally rare spring sandwort *(Minuartia verna)*. Other associates were even smaller, like the ephemeral spring whitlow-grass, parsley piert and annual and sea pearlworts.

A typical neighbour was the yellow-flowered biting stonecrop or wall pepper. This is a lime-lover, unlike the pinky-white flowered English stonecrop, which shows a distinct preference for the more acid soils of anthills on Aran. Another was cat's-foot or mountain everlasting *(Antennaria dioica)*, with its pink or

55. Mountain Everlasting, or Cat's Foot

99

white flower heads and creeping runners beset with silvery furred leaves.

Different patterns of jointing and erosion produce broad, vertical sided clints or narrow elongated ones stretching away interminably across the tableland. The separating grykes range from several inches to several feet in depth but are seldom more than a foot wide. This is a classic limestone pavement, with few plants venturing out into the merciless drying winds and within reach of hungry herbivores.

Woody plants like blackthorn and juniper turn their twigs at right angles on reaching into the daylight, to grow on in a flattened tangle of branches, cleaving to the rock surface and affording each other mutual shelter. Their above ground behaviour is not the only factor ensuring their survival. The food store contained within the seed is crucial. A seed dropping into a deep crevice has to be able to maintain the young plant on its passage up through the darkness until it reaches the light and becomes self sufficient.

Much the showiest flowers of the grykes as April advanced into May were bloody cranesbill, roseroot and burnet rose. We saw no less than eleven members of the Geranium family on the island, nine cranesbills and two storksbills. Ones often associated with the most colourful of them all were the shining, the Pyrenean and herb Robert. Dovesfoot, small-flowered and purple cranesbills associated with the uncommon sticky storksbill along sandy shorelines, cut-leaved and two-flowered cranesbills with common storksbill by waysides and wall bases.

Roseroot *(Sedum roseum)* is a special beauty, both inland with hemp agrimony and valerian and on clifftops with rock samphire and sea beet. It is named for the scent of roses which wafts from newly injured rootstocks.

Much larger than most of our native stonecrops, the notched, fleshy, sometimes rose tinted leaves are broadly flattened, the terminal ones forming a rosette around the massed yellow flowers. Male and female blooms are separate. In the male eight purple-tipped stamens extend beyond the four yellow petals around aborted female organs. Fruits ripening in the female are frequently orange.

Burnet rose, often in association with wood sage, may emerge from apparently soil-less jumbles of rock fragments. Straying beyond the grykes are drifts of hoary rock rose *(Helianthemum canum)*, much the rarer of our two unspotted rock roses and one which is associated with bloody cranesbill on the Carboniferous Limestone cliffs of Gower in South

Wales. Aran and the Burren are apparently its only Irish sites.

Bristly wild madder, bittersweet and creeping cinquefoil favour beaches as well as grykes, wood sanicle, greater willow herb and pignut are also at home in the limited hazel spinneys.

Cliffs dropping almost vertically to the sea can suffer douchings with salt water right to the summit. Their crevices contain plants from the very different medium of salt marsh, notably sea Aster, sea milkwort, sea plantain and scurvy grass. With them are the more to be expected crevice plants of rock samphire, sea campion, sea mayweed and thrift. A few salt-tolerant species from the back of the broad sandy beaches, like sea radish also withstand these conditions. Sprouting boldly from ledges are occasional tall tree mallow or Alexanders plants.

Other Umbellifers to be found in grykes are wild carrot, burnet saxifrage and Scottish lovage *(Ligusticum scoticum)* with shining leaves resembling those of Angelica.

No account of gryke vegetation would be complete without mention of the many ferns, some grossly attenuated as they reach out to the light from hidden depths. The usually chunky rusty-back fern can attain frond lengths of twelve inches or more, while the delicate maidenhair fern, so

56. Scottish Lovage

familiar in greenhouses, can reach to twice that. This last is a southern species, centred in the Mediterranean and Tropics, but pioneering plants managed to move north as the ice retreated to colonise cliffs in Devon, Cornwall and South Wales as well as Ireland.

Conversely, the usually rumbustious bracken seldom attains its normal potential, being browned off and cut short by gales, although not often grazed. Hart's tongue ferns are probably the most characteristic, uncurling long green tongues into the daylight. Both polypodies are present, the larger *Polypodium interjectum* in shady crevices, the smaller *Polypodium vulgare* in sunnier sites.

Four spleenworts occur, sea spleenwort doing particularly well on the western cliffs. Shining fronds of black spleenwort and delicate ones of maidenhair spleenwort sprout alongside the smaller, neater wall rue, which sometimes grows with the not dissimilar rue-leaved saxifrage.

Each day took us to different areas and what a range of sites there was to visit in so small a compass. Most dramatic were the massive ancient forts, built stone upon stone by muscular people of the Bronze and Iron Ages. They occur on all three of the islands, their walls incredibly thick. Were the three populations at war with each other or did they unite against a common foe? Or, more imminently, were the occupants of the three forts on Inishmore at war with each other for the slender available resources?

The stone piles seemed impregnable, their walls unscalable. The labour that went into their construction and the fear that stimulated this were difficult to conceive. Surely the making of soil to grow scanty crops on marginal sites providing few game animals should have been enough!

These people are believed to have been linked with the Belgic Celts, their colossal constructions regarded as among the most important in Europe. We could not but compare their durability favourably with the Iron Age forts ranged along the cliffs of Glamorgan's Heritage Coast. Those had been built of timber, a material probably not available to the Aran Islanders, and all that remains today are the circular earth banks on which the defensive palisades were erected.

Dun Aengus, built around 1300, stands 285 ft (87m) above the sea on a sheer north-western cliff. Like the Welsh ones, this and others were ranged along the coast, the perpendicularity of the cliffs a natural defence against invaders from the sea. The great walls curved inland and back to the cliff edge. They were supported by hefty stone buttresses added later during nineteenth century renovations, and the passage through for humans was scanty.

Clambering over the remains we were most impressed by the cheval-de-frise (plural chevaux-de-frise) spreading across the landward approach to deter attackers. A less closely jumbled version was used later in Europe to thwart cavalry. Mounted warriors were no threat on Aran, nor in the modern version which is defined as: "A defensive obstacle composed of barbed wire on spikes attached to a wooden frame or jagged glass or spikes set in the masonry on top of a wall."

The Aran version needed to be built of stone, like everything else. Narrow slabs were set with their lower ends firmly wedged in crevices, their sharp tops sloping out towards any approaching enemy. Too closely aligned and staggered to allow men to pass easily between, they would yet give insufficient cover for men to creep through unseen..

Dun Eochla, the fort of the yew wood, is sited inland on the side of the hill west of Cilronan Bay. It boasts concentric, two tier walls some eighteen feet high inside the outer defences. The solid stone tower in the centre had been erected in the nineteenth century when remains of the original clochans or beehive dwelling huts were dismantled. This, like the building of the many field walls, was the easiest way of disposing of excess rock in a land consisting of little else. Some of us scrambled up on top and prostrated ourselves in the sunshine like sacrificial offerings on an altar.

Dun Dubh Chathair, Ducathair or the Black Fort lies on the south-west coast opposite Cilronan Bay, south-east of Dun Aengus and on a much lower cliff. It retains a pattern of low walls, these the bases of former living accommodation comprising a close huddle of oval stone huts on land enclosed between the protective battlements and the cliff edge. Flights of steps served the two levels on the seaward side of the sixteen foot high, five metre thick outer wall.

This is thought to be from the late Iron Age, built around five hundred AD. It occupies a protruding headland, the wall stretching from cliff to cliff needed to be but a foreshortened semi-circle. The higher of the two levels reaches to about the same height as the last and the cheveaux de frise of sharpened stone slabs stretches the whole

of its length.. Nearby is the much more modern lighthouse and coastguard station, abandoned because it was so often lost in the clouds and useless to navigators. There is a fourth fort which we failed to investigate.

57. Milk Vetch and Pyramidical Bugle

Stones in the fort walls were too neatly slotted together to harbour much plant life, but there was no shortage of botanical interest round about.. Two unfamiliar species by Dun Aengus were purple milk vetch *(Astragalus danicus)* and pyramidal bugle *(Ajuga pyramidalis)*.

We encountered the milk vetch again in turf bordering the eastern sands, but it is not found on the Burren, Aran being its only Irish station. The sands are as calcareous as the rocks, being composed partly of flaky shell fragments like those across the water around Bunowen Pier. The vetch is rare in our latitude, being found mainly in Scotland.

Pyramidal bugle is a plant of Central European mountains, including the Alps, but also occurs sparsely on limestone rocks in Scotland, Westmorland and Clare, Galway and Rathlin Island in Eire.

From Dun Eochla a partly grassed track took us past a ruined clochan or beehive store hut and a scrap of marsh dominated by shoots of purple loosestrife spearing up from a sward of angled marsh foxtail grass. Narrow-leaved bog cotton would be conspicuous here when the fruits fluffed out among flowering water mint in autumn.

Our track ended at Pointe Fiain, from where we reached the coast with few obstacles. Fierce waves buffeted flat slabs under the headland, rolling on to discharge their energy into a blowhole. Their awesome boom added spice to our lunch sandwiches as we settled near the chasm, which dropped vertically through two hundred feet of rock to sea level. A "Halt" notice appeared, rather too close to be entirely effective.

The white spume below was framed by the circle of thrift around the brink and we could visualise spray shooting right up through the 'puffing' hole in rough weather, to baptise the intrepid vegetable fringe.

Poll na Brioscarnach Rock Arch on this south coast lay just beyond to the east, soapsuds swirling round its base like the bow wave of a high rigged ship on a frustrated voyage to nowhere. Cliffs here were seriously undercut by these ferocious tides, but the overhangs looked too massive to be in any danger of falling.

We edged round a few wall ends, padded across ice-scraped levels and high-stepped over rocks and grikes to reach the Black Fort. A rather scummy stream, hopefully not the ancient inmates' water supply, was subjected to enough blown sea salt to be occupied by green strings (Enteromorpha) and other green algae, with no freshwater plants.

58. *Sea Arrow and Least Soft Brome Grass*

Tall sea arrow grass *(Triglochin maritima)* had ascended far beyond its normal saltmarsh level here, under the influence of the flying spray, but the sea plantain swards were not so extensive on these cliffs as on those of Inishbofin.

The thrift community topping the headland that rebuffed the boisterous tides, sheltered another two unusual plant species. One, the stone bramble *(Rubus saxatilis)*, had narrow white petals dwarfed by the larger sepals and would produce shining raspberry-like fruits in due season. The other was the chunky little seaside brome grass *(Bromus hordeaceus ssp. ferronii)*.

Two dry valleys near the Black Fort were lined with such lush grass that we suspected a surface water seepage. This was confirmed when we came across a stone-bordered well reaching down to the water table. Used now for watering livestock, it would no doubt have proved vital to inmates of the ancient stronghold. The name An Turloch Mor on the map suggests a more obvious body of water.

A grassy path led us past the Four Beauties Church and another to the auk colonies. Kittiwakes, fulmars and guillemots nested on the under-pinning cliffs, their incessant calls wafting eerily up on rising air currents. Had their forebears contributed to Iron Age meals, we wondered? Some probably had, but not the fulmars which did not start moving down from Scotland until many centuries later.

A few black guillemots rested on a central rock between fishing bouts, that were likely to be in pursuit of butterfish rather than the sand eels that were favoured by other birds of their size. Razorbills rafted on the sea, but there were no puffins. It was not their sort of island. Puffins burrow in soil to nest and there is very little of that life-giving commod-ity to spare on Aran.

By no means all the terrain was barren rockscape. One end of the island was a green tapestry of quite large fields with fewer walls. These and the little grazing paddocks of the rest, dissected by walled lanes, provided a much kindlier landscape. Here were bright swards of buttercups and field daisies nestled among familiar grasses like sweet vernal, cocksfoot, soft brome and quaking grass or shivery-shakes.

Some were more characteristic of mountain sheep pastures, with a range of fine-leaved fescues and blue moor grass *(Sesleria caerulea)*, which is a mountain plant in most of Europe. Accompanying milkwort flowers shone as brightly blue as the spring gentians among the more sombre violets and no less than seven species of speedwell. Dark tufts of black bog rush *(Schoenus nigricans)* contrasted with the fresh, cucumber-scented leaves of salad burnet.

These little paddocks were the domain of the wild orchids. Early purple and green-winged orchids were at their prime by the end of May and the more bulbous bee orchid flowers were just bursting from their sheaths. Pyramidal and common spotted orchids were yet to offer their goodies to the insect world, while twayblade and autumn lady's tresses orchids would mature later.

Brighter than these last were yellow pea, yellow rattle, slender St. John's wort and lady's mantle, pierced by a few spikes of great mullein. Flecks of pink were contributed by centaury and mallow with more extensive sweeps of red clover.

59. Irish Eyebright, Thyme Broomrape and Thyme

105

Irish eyebright *(Euphrasia salisburgiensis)* was so closely associated with the mats of thyme that those probably provided the hosts for these partial parasites. A non-green plant completely dependent on the thyme for sustenance was thyme broomrape. This had deep red stems, scales leaves and flowers, but masqueraded under the name of *Orobanche alba*.

Red, white and blue along waysides and wall bases were supplied by long-headed poppies, dame's violet and clary *(Papaver dubium, Hesperis matronalis* and *Salvia horminoides)*. Columbine or granny's bonnet may have escaped from gardens, like the Spanish bluebells. True English bluebells were surprisingly absent - as were their frequent associates, red campion. Harebells, knotted pearlwort and rock cress *(Arabis hirsuta)* were mostly tucked away in crevices.

Sea and field mouse-ear chickweeds *(Cerastium diffusum* and *C. arvense)* helped to clothe open patches, along with the two stiff little grasses, Desmazeria or Catapodium. Requiring more shelter were greater burnet saxifrage and wild carrot.

Some spathes of lords and ladies or Jack-in-the-pulpit had been chomped off by sheep or goats seeking the starch-rich maroon spadix within. This wild Arum encroaches into the most sheltered habitat of all - the tumbled, terraced woodlands, which more resemble its traditional home. Ivy clambered over the vertical rock faces like an upended version of the usual ivy ground cover of heavily shaded woods.

Honeysuckle pushed out into the fresh air at its peril and the more woody nestled close to the massive silvered strata. Hazel was much the commonest, with sycamore, elder and a little spindle and dogwood.

Surprisingly the sturdy, polished leaves of holly proved little more resistant to salt than deciduous ones. Mature leaves had frequently been shed to be replaced by tufts of newly sprouted yellow-green ones, tightly bunched for mutual protection in a plucky effort to make ammends. Tiny leaves of juniper had fared better.

Pink-flowered dog roses clawed their way up through the knobbly twigs, along with well armed brambles, this less at home in the grykes than the creamy-white flowered burnet roses that we so often associete with sand dunes.

One of the five willows identified, the creeping willow, is also more often encountered on dunes. We spotted an almond-leaved willow *(Salix triandra)* in an alder spinney, while osiers sprang up readily among grey and goat sallows.

Understorey herbs were hard put to it to find enough light in the dense tangle, but primroses were to be found among queen Ann's lace. Others were ramsons or wild garlic, its pungent white flowers followed by those of meadowsweet and nipplewort.

Knowing how porous and crevassed the limestone is, we were surprised at how many wetland sites we came across during our wanderings. One such was a grass-green temporary pond nestled in a long valley. This proved to be a turlough or seasonal lake, filling with the rising water table of winter and draining away into the bedrock in summer.

The rocky floors of turloughs visited on the mainland were blackened by a mantle of *Cinclidotus fontinaloides* moss advancing over the boulders of the floor and up among the stumps of marginal shrubs, but I recall seeing none of that here.

A small heronry was sited alongside, the nests crowded in low bushes growing on ledges just above the water. Gawky youngsters, ranging in size from small and naked to larger and untidily wispy, wove naked necks in empty air as if to hustle another consignment of food back to the nest. There can be few creatures more raggedly dishevelled and ugly than a juvenile heron.

It is more usual for us to find herons nesting in the tops of tall trees, as near to the sky as they can get. I have, however, seen a number of heronries

60. Grey Heron at nest

on stunted bushes in the dry Tropics, on coral islands and even on rock ledges above the treeline in Scotland, where I looked down into the nest contents instead of up to their twiggy bases.

Herons are as adaptable as ospreys, which build stacks of ground-based twigs on coral reefs in Australia, more elegant piles on telegraph poles in the Southern USA and windworthy structures on the tops of pines in Scotland.

A little reedbed had developed at one end of Aran's mini turlough and a stand of sea club rush at the other. Water bistort sprouted from the dwindling water between - this a plant capable of producing both floating leaves and tougher sub-aerial ones as the habitat demanded.

Elegant sandwich terns floated across the pool and a tail-bobbing common sandpiper flew from shore to shore, whistling evocatively, as in our Welsh mountains. A curlew passed low along the horizon and the air was full of hurtling swifts.

Near the pretty thatched village of Gort nag Gapull was an extensive plot wholly under water and full of bogbean *(Menyanthes trifoliata)* in full flower. A sprinkling of buttercups and spearwort mingled with the tousled pink and white blooms and emergent sweeps' brushes of horsetail. The milkmaids or lady's smocks of May would give way to meadowsweet, water mint and purple loosestrife. Two withy beds snuggled into the foot of the encircling cliff, which was backed by a few cottages

Nearby we were able to watch a basket maker at work, cloth cap pulled down over his eyes and legs gaitered with waterproof plastic sacks for kneeling in damp grass among the buttercups and daisies. He was fashioning a large storage basket, or kreel, for potatoes, turf or fish. Different shapes cater for nets and long lines to be reeled out over the stern of the fishing boats or as panniers to fit over the backs of patient donkeys.

The stout, eight foot tall uprights, known locally as sallies, had their butt ends rammed into the turf in groups of three or four to form a square, finer, more supple withies being woven back and forth between the groups. A narrow gap was left amidships, presumably for ease of lifting when full. The uprights were chopped off a few inches above the top instead of being bent over and woven into the rim.

This technique was not used for lobster pots, which came in two main patterns. Cylindrical ones were made of wooden laths bound together by circles of split hazel rods such as might be used to skewer thatch to a roof. Others, of slightly stouter timber, were half cylinders on a flat base, swathed in stout red fishing net to prevent the trapped crustaceans escaping between the more widely spread bars. Only the ends were netted in the others.

On a walk to Kilmurvey Bay, lingering to watch wheatears leaving and entering a nest in a sand-backed wall, we turned up a leafy lane to where a spring emerged from an aquifer into a covered, stone-lined well.

The clear water was swarming with Gammarid freshwater shrimps, a good indication of its purity. It opened out into a sizable limestone basin with common gnats *(Culex pipiens)* laying eggs and pond skaters sculling over the surface where this was not disrupted by emergent watercress. Marginal Eleocharis spike rush and black sedge mingled with eruptions of greater bird's foot trefoil backed by soldierly Timothy grass.

We followed a seepage line past water starwort and three kinds of willow-herb to a smooth spread of bright green Marchantia liverwort, its gemmae cups brimming with tiny green reproductive discs waiting to be wafted away to spawn new plants. A little further on, beyond a stand of wood melick, was an alder spinney with quite sizable trees, including a few ashes, this backed by flowering gorse.

Larger bodies of water served as reservoirs, although quite a number of households still depended on wells or springs. Supplies were never lavish, the flawed limestone allowing much of the quite adequate rainfall to seep away. Recently motor-driven pumps had been installed to pipe this vital commodity from the clifftop reservoir near Dun Aengus to the rest.

The end of the island wholly carpeted with large grass fields was furnished with neatly effective drinking troughs having piled stones alongside serving as a sloping catchment area for rain. Older troughs had a thin coating of cement over the catchment and trough lining, this more generous in newer, larger ones, where the trough appeared to be wholly of concrete, probably over breeze blocks.

Coastal lagoons trapped behind shingle bars were ineffective as water supplies, except, perhaps, for the more tolerant livestock, their large area and low elevation leading to contamination by sea water. One such in the north of the island lay adjacent to the prime grazing fields. The enclosing storm bank had advanced from near a cluster of houses at the side of a former bay to join up with a low rocky point protruding where the coast turned sharply at a right angle.

As in other such lagoons, thick drifts of Enteromorpha billowed around the stems of emergent brackish and freshwater plants, principally water bistort. It seemed likely that the bulk of the enclosed water was dominated by beaked tasselweed *(Ruppia maritima)* as thick banks of this had drifted onto the leeward shore, some thrown up over the low bordering wall by wavelets.

The seaside version of what has been traditionally known as the true bullrush, but now the common clubrush, was advancing out into the lagoon on a broad front. These shorter, greyer

61. Beaked Tasselweed and Enteromorpha

plants are known as grey clubrush *(Schoenoplectus tabernaemontani)* now that the Typha reedmace or cattail has usurped the name of bulrush that the two formerly shared.

Opposite, on the landward side of the confining storm beach, was a similar, greener bed of another of these sedgy plants caught up in the recent name changes. Formerly sea sedge *(Scirpus maritimus)*, this now goes under the name of sea clubrush *(Bolboschoenus maritimus)*. Sea Aster burgeoned along its lower margin and a reed bed had established nearby.

The crest of the confining shingle bar was occupied by rock samphire with a little sea beet and bittersweet. The seaward slope was still mobile and bare. The landward slope nurtured sea campion and pellitory-of-the-wall. Where sand accumulated lower down were chunky little 'four square' shoots of sea sandwort *(Honkenya peploides)*, spilling little green 'peas' onto the sand. With it were sea mayweed, bird's-foot trefoil and fescue grass.

A pair of mute swans on the lagoon had two charming cygnets in tow. Five drake mallard were sunning themselves on the water, but only one duck, in charge of two ducklings. We suspected that another four ducks might be tucked away on their nests, hatching out more recruits. Two decorative sheldrakes sailed the waters while another was out on the bay where the grey seals lolled.

Four herons stalked the shallows, jabbing occasionally at fish, while a little grebe dived for others. A single moorhen was pulling trails of green algae from the depths. Three dunlins, wearing the black underbelly of their summer plumage, were a welcome sight, as we usually see these birds only in winter. Two lapwings, two curlews and an expostulating oyster catcher completed the wader tally - these out on the salty side of the spit, where gulls and terns were sampling the shallows for small fry.

Near Kilronan was a smaller brackish pool and beyond it a lochan, the salt-tolerant element here represented by sea milkwort, sea arrow-grass and saltmarsh or mud rush *(Juncus gerardi)* with beaked tasselweed in the outlet stream.

Possum shrimps, with eyes out on side stalks, spurted from the green algae, with which they seemed wholly compatible. Fawn coloured Corixid water boatmen, probably too large for Plea, seemed wholly out of context, but increased upstream in the sweeter water flowing from the lochan.

To the few pond skaters salinity levels must have seemed less important, their widely splayed feet scarcely dimpling the surface film as they scudded about their business picking off waterlogged midges.

The little black spire snails were probably *Hydrobia ventrosa*, a species at home in brackish lagoons having no direct contact with the sea and withstanding less saltiness than the commoner laver spire snails (*Hydrobia ulvae*) of estuarine mud. We had found more of the same in a brackish clifftop stream two hundred feet above the sea near Dun Aengus. The whorls of the long tapered shells are more rounded than in the salt water species.

Over marginal vegetation long-headed flies (Dolichopus), with shining bottle-green bodies, were copulating, pick-a-back style as a break from preying on smaller flies and aphids.

It was bank holiday Sunday, third of June, when we explored Kilronan Bay, the big event of the day being the curragh racing. Craft used for this purpose lacked the tip-tilted prows which enabled the traditional sea-going curraghs to breast oncoming waves so successfully during the launch. Racing was not attempted in that sort of sea. Nevertheless, the only crews we saw were all male, unlike those partaking in the gig races of other island groups such as the Scillies and Channel Islands.

62. *Donkeys and ponies on the sandflats*

Vast expanses of sand were exposed hereabouts on the ebb. A great circular patch filled with water as the tide rose, but sand spits were advancing to close the entrance and create yet another brackish lagoon in days to come.

Sand not inundated at high tide was subjected to wind blow, piling up in rolling dunes that we were to see more of on Inisheer. The eastern part was accreting and being stabilised by vigorous marram grass in the natural course of plant succession. Beyond the airfield, where little planes landed on the sand flats that filled much of the partially enclosed bay, a regiment of marram shoots had been planted to stabilise the periphery and prevent loose sand blowing over the hard landing ground.

The area was currently fenced with wire mesh to keep livestock out, but the contingent of ten donkeys that had taken lunch with us on the beach squeezed through the iron gate, which stood ajar, to partake of the lush grass and legumes on the other side as afters. They were eminently

111

sociable donkeys, showing no particular preference as to what they ate. Their manners were impeccable, just a gentle nuzzling with velvet noses to remind us of their needs and a patient wait while apples were peeled. or crusts removed. Only the horse that shared their free range quarters and joined in the mutual preening sessions remained aloof.

The extent of sand movement, both building up and blowing away, was ably demonstrated in the shorescape. An ancient church, now waist deep in vegetated sand, had apparently been completely buried before being dug out. The masons of old had not heeded the biblical passage about shifting sands!

Animals were excluded, so that this and the extensive graveyard round about had become covered by a protective mantle of green. Dune pioneers, such as the long, straight lines of sand sedge and sprawling sea Convolvulus with its gay pink trumpet flowers, were being superceded by grass, legumes and composites.

Stone monuments like sentry boxes topped by sturdy crosses bordered the road, where it would have been hard to dig graves without dynamite. They were the shape and size of coffins, but I was assured there were no standing up corpses inside. (Above ground interment may be the norm in thermal areas, where conditions below ground are inappropriately hot, so why not here?)

The air strip was sandwiched between the tidal sand flats and the first low rock terraces covered by accreting sand. Once the marram grass had eliminated sand blow, flowering plants came romping across the spaces between tufts. Some added stability with runners or rhizomes, some with ground hugging rosettes, all with deep roots seeking out the errant moisture.

Yellow was the predominant colour, with bird's-foot trefoil forming the matrix. Kidney vetch, meadow vetchling, lesser yellow trefoil and black medick added their quota of soil nitrates to that captured by the dominant. There was yellow-wort with its wierd, stem-embracing leaves and yellow rattle, its inflated capsules vibrating with unattached seeds.

Crimson runners escaped from creeping cinquefoil and silverweed and mealy white ones from mouse-ear hawkweed. Rosettes

63. Yellow Wort and Yellow Rattle

112

of various magnitude sprouted plantain spikes, carline thistle heads and yellow daisies - other hawkweeds, hawkbits, cat's-ear. dandelion and ragwort.

Most delightful were the drifts of sea pansies *(Viola tricolor).* Lacking the purple petals which are so often present, these were strictly bicolour, in two shades of yellow. Nevertheless, they constituted grave ornaments more decorative than many of the contrived ones and spilled out across the sand. Later in the year they would be succeeded by yellow bedstraw.

In early summer broad mats of bulbous buttercups had produced a number of sports. Some flowers were double the normal size, with as many as twelve petals and a few were twinned. Danish milk vetch grew at the seaward margin of plant life here with seedlings of prickly saltwort and older specimens of the annual hastate and frosted oraches. Scarlet pimpernel flowers were predominantly an apricot pink.

64. *Prickly Saltwort and Frosted Orache*

Larks carolled overhead, trilling a requiem for the dear departed, and the strains of a cuckoo wafted across the sands. Swallows scooped up insects come to sip nectar from the flowery sward or prey on those which had. Meadow pipits and starlings were everywhere on the dunes, the latter straying into the little port. Most of the whitewashed houses there were roofed with slates, as often in the outlying villages, where their thatched forebears had been relegated for use as barns. Ridge tiles provided fine songposts for the starling's skilful mimicry of those around.

We watched a song thrush smashing snails on the rock standings of the sentinel box monuments, the surounding dunes offering no substrate suitably hard. And there was no shortage of snails, with all that limestone and shell sand for shell building.

The notoriously varied Cepaea hedge snails were predominantly black and white humbug striped here, some as large as the equally abundant Helix garden snails. Thrushes had no need to make inroads into the liberally scattered but much smaller Planorbis type Helicellas and others.

Wheatears frequented both the dune draped backing rocks and sand sufficiently stable to accommodate rabbit burrows in which they might find nesting sites. They cohabited well with rabbits, foraging more successfully over their closely nibbled swards than in the lusher growths inside the airfield's supposedly stock-proof fence.

Lapwings were most at home on the sandflats, wrens, robins and blackbirds around the settlement with its tiny gardens, Fuchsias, Escallonias and even the odd New Zealand cabbage tree (Cordyline). Turnstones and curlews favoured the beach. Jackdaws were not chimney pot birds here, as in the Welsh Valleys. They were away with the choughs or red-legged daws chacking around the walls of the ancient forts.

With so many flowers offering nectar for the taking, there was no short-age of insects. Overwintering brimstone butterflies were still about, along with large and small whites and orange tips from the spring 'hatch-ing'. Small tortoiseshells were mating, as were common blues, preparing for the next brood.

Already the first of the flickering summer hordes of meadow browns were emerging, while the more distinctively marked wall browns had not far to seek a wall for their favourite pastime of sun-bathing. Small heaths were on the wing and the even more cryptic small blues, along with a suspected brown argus.

Lackey moth caterpillars were mostly at an early stage of develop-ment. Small furry brown ones clustered together on stout silken webs of their own making. Larger larvae in a later instar were more widely dispersed among the frasse of their discarded skins. None had yet reached the more adventurous blue, orange and white striped phase.

A solitary, three inch long, darkly hirsute caterpillar with oblique white flashes proved to be that of a drinker moth. Fluttery burnet companion moths and carpet moths were on the wing, the narrow Crambe grass moths were as somnolent as always, until brushed from their perch by a passer-by.

A splendid female emperor moth had just emerged from her cocoon and was clinging beneath a flower cluster pumping fluid into the veins of her wings, until those were spread in all their glory, complete with peacock tail eye spots. Soon she would be broadcasting her 'come hither' pheromones to entice the more brightly coloured but smaller males to have their way with her. Although often feeding on heather, the fat spotted caterpillars are equally at home on hawthorn, willow and bramble leaves. A neatly opened acorn shaped moth cocoon nearby had housed a moth smaller than the emperor.

We were fortunate to come across the unmistakable rose chafer scarab beetle *(Cetonia aurata)* feeding on the petals of a burnet rose protruding from a gryke. Indeterminate yellow lines wavered across the broad, glossy green back of this imposing beetle, which is more likely to be seen in the Mediterranean than Britain nowadays. Responding to the urge to

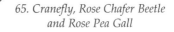

65. Cranefly, Rose Chafer Beetle and Rose Pea Gall

fly to another rose, it freed its wings for flight with the elytra or wing cases closed, an unusual feat among beetles.

Much smaller but still glossy green were the leaf beetles munching exclusively on their selected leaves. Seven spot ladybirds were munching on aphids. Green and russet shield bugs rested on a dwarfed hawthorn and black and yellow striped hoverflies hung suspended in front of flowers, quite motionless except for the rapidly vibrating wings. St. Marks flies were still with us, swarming in the sunshine.

Craneflies were mating, tail to tail. Rising from their patch of buttercups they flew in tandem, the plumper female, with broad yellow stripes travelling forwards while the more slender male with orange stripes was being hauled along backwards, although still flapping his wings in fine style.

There is a special Aran bee, but the ones we were finding were common red-tailed bumble bees *(Bombus lapidarius).* An ichneumon wasp was identified by a museum expert as probably *Peltocarus dentatus,* but there are half a dozen other possibles in the same tribe.

Some of Aran's Hymenopterans (of the bee:wasp fraternity) were invisible, their presence manifested only by the plants in which they chose to live. One such species was the gall wasp *Diplolepis eglanteriae,* which caused scarlet pea galls to bulge from rose leaflets. These were smooth. A closely related species produces spiked pea galls, like miniature naval mines. Each 'pea' contains a single individual, as egg, larva and pupa. They had been produced earlier in the season than normal and would fall to the ground in autumn for a flying adult to emerge in spring. And then, of course, there were ants, black, brown and yellow.

Not all of Inishmore's coastline was as sandy as the donkeys' grazing flats or as precipitous as the Dun Aengus cliffs. There were pleasant in

115

between sites of more accessible rocky shore with salty tidal pools to dabble in.

One such was the so-called Poll na bPeist "Serpent Hole", which we visited at high and low tides. This natural rectangular reservoir of sea water had Atlantic rollers breaking in over the barrier at high water and siphoning in through a tunnel at low.

The surrounding cliffs were an amalgam of smooth terraces and piled boulders well supplied with calcite veins and fossils. We moved to a lower level to appreciate more fully the waves infiltrating crannies and spurting out in jets and fountains of spray. Low tide would be more appropriate for swimming.

A few ringed plovers and oyster catchers and the odd curlew rested on the bleak rock pavement alongside, the first two species showing signs of nesting closeby.

On the turf above were spherical *Bovista plumbea* puffballs with no sterile base. These were fresh, the outer white skin not yet peeled to reveal the membrane surrounding the dark, lead coloured spore ball. The English name of grey puffball embraces the two colour phases, neither quite accurately. Nearby were some shrivelled fairy ring fungi *(Marasmius oreades)* and further inland some freshly emerged St. George's mushrooms *(Tricholoma gambosum).*

66. Faery Ring Fungus, St. George's Mushroom and Puffball

Sea level slabs explored at the north end of the island were highly fossiliferous. Commonest were Brachiopods, like big bivalves with fewer coiled Goniatite univalves. Some of the eroding colonial corals were several feet across, these sometimes flooring rock pools, as their substance was worn away more readily than the surrounding unreconstituted limestone. The wave-smoothed surface of these cut across the central branches of the colony transversely and the marginally radiating ones obliquely.

The beadlet anemones were familiar enough, but the spherical sea urchins were *Paracentrotus lividus,* found almost exclusively in Western Ireland except for a spillover in Devon and Cornwall and an outlier in the Hebrides. Their calcified tests were an olive green, their radiating spines long, sharply pointed and purple. Often clustered together, these bore holes in the rocks.

Ash tray sized scallop shells had washed up from deeper levels but the transfixed mussels were small. Pink painted top shells, orange smooth periwinkles and yellowish rough periwinkles lay around among the limpets. More mobile were shrimps and sea slaters of various sizes, these last scampering over the rocks on their many legs or swimming just as efficiently. An old treetrunk shorn of its bark had been riddled by teredo borers, making it useless as timber other than for fuel. In the absence of peat, the main fuel used at the time was coal brought in by steamer and canisters of bottled gas.

On the more exposed west end of the island Irish sea urchins were abundant in mid tide pools among velvety sprays of Codium. With them were small hermit crabs in the shells of edible winkles and unhoused shore crabs. Shell middens scattered along the shore were mostly of edible winkles or limpets.

Living limpets were rasping away audibly at algal spores and sporelings under the ledges. These have been dubbed the rabbits of the seashore. Destroy them, as by the "Sea Empress" oil spill off South-west Wales in 1996, and formerly almost bare rock becomes covered by large green algae and then brown wracks in the normal course of succession. Both these plant covers are largely eliminated as the limpets recover their numbers and get busy scraping up the germinating spores once more.

Seaweeds included three edible ones, brown tang (Alaria), red dulse (Rhodymenia) and red caragheen (Chondrus rather than Gigartina). Other brown algae were Scytosiphon, like strings of sausages, Halidrys with pointed air bladders and filmentous Ectocarpous, other reds included Nitophyllum and calcified Corallina.

67. *Scytosiphon, Halidrys and Nitophyllum seaweeds*

The more mobile element here included shrimps, both normal and opossum with stalked eyes. The most obvious pool fish were gobies, their pelvic fins united to form a sucker, enabling them to cling to the pool floor and withstand wave break.

Moving around in small groups as we did, it was customary at appropriate hours to be good tourists and knock on a cottage door with a request for a pot of tea. In so doing we met many interesting characters.

One such was an island nurse married to a farmer with sixteen acres of mostly poor land on which he kept a cow and calf, two young steers, a pony and trap and the usual hens and ducks. Her four children, sons and daughters, had all won scholarships to mainland schools and gone on to university or teacher training college. Currently they were living in New York, Boston, Washington and Australia. Mother had, herself, spent six weeks in New York. She told us that many of the islanders spend much of their working lives in the United States but return to Aran in their retirement.

It is not only the merchant seamen in this supposedly remote island community who get around to see a deal more of the big wide world than most ordinary mortals on the supposedly more accessible mainland. This is a case of "Necessity drives". In the old days there was nothing to come back to, said our nursing acquaintance. Now, by the 1970s, there was prosperity, mostly in fishing and building, with new houses springing up everywhere. This is a long way from the insular, poverty stricken state of many islands in the past. Long may their good fortune continue, with most of the toil of making soil to eke out a living but a distant memory.

INISHEER

Exploration of the delightful island of Inisheer was relegated to day trips: one in June 1979 and another twenty seven years later in June 2006. No landing facilities for large sea-going craft were available on the smaller islands in the 1970s and our crossing from Inishmore in a small fishing boat took an hour and ten minutes. Fluffy cloudlets scudded across the bluest of blue skies and the sun shone benignly on a sea as calm as the Atlantic can ever be.

The modest stone quay and cluster of cottages was once again backed by a vast acreage of sand flats. Part had been fenced off from livestock, stabilised by limestone chippings and sown with perennial rye grass and clovers, as an airfield. The narrow runway was bordered by half tyres, painted white and a small 'plane came gliding in smoothly between them as we watched.

The air link had been established about six years earlier and the current motley of donkey-powered jaunting car, motorised van and light aircraft characterised life styles of past, present and future all rolled into one. Modernisation, including the generation of electricity, lagged behind that on the larger island.

Only part of the surrounding flats was livestock-free, the contrast between the protected, flower decked sward in sharp contrast to the donkey-denuded sand alongside. Fencing was the essential first component of any land reclamation scheme. The resulting sward could be used either for grazing when root systems were sufficiently well entrenched to withstand modest animal pressure, or ploughed back in as green manuring to give body to a soil destined to carry richer swards or even arable crops. Almost the first comers were legumes, able to capture atmospheric nitrogen to enhance the system.

So far this had not happened on a big scale but a pocket sized example of what was possible could be seen in an old cottage garden, which must formerly have been fenced. Purple Irises and orange wallflowers grew along the base of the one protective wall and the central 'lawn' area was a spontaneous sward of grass and bird's-foot trefoil more colourful than many a formal garden ashore. Marginal erosion showed darker humus accumulated in the top few inches, contrasting with the white sand below.

Obscure outlines of old fields around the ancient forts and rumours of the former existence of trees, suggested that the whole island might once have had similar organic fertility - long since eroded from the flat limestone as surely as this turf was being eroded from the flat sands. This is the old story of desertification by over cultivation and animal husbandry in the presence of punishing winds.

A more recent experiment had been set up in the 1970s well in from the shore near the top of the great beach where the island curraghs were made and mended. Rows of marram grass shoots had been planted along both margins of fenced plots. The more short-lived plot showed a ridge building up on the seaward side, the grass thrusting up through the accumulated sand that it had arrested in passing. The remainder of the area was almost as bald as before.

The older experimental plot showed a lofty, fully vegetated ridge along the seaward flank and a lower one facing the land. Fleshy sea spurge (*Euphorbia paralias*) and bird's-foot trefoil were conspicuous with more marram between. Spontaneous incomers were ribwort plantain, dandelion and ragwort, all holding patches of sand with their spreading leaf rosettes.

68. Sea Spurge, Sand Couch and Sea Counch

Other grasses resembled marram in their grey-green reflective surfaces but were less effective as sand binders. They are sand couch and sea couch, recently renamed *Elytrigia juncea* and *Elytrigia atherica*. The sand couch is able to withstand inundation by salt water and grows to seaward of the sea couch, in spite of their unfortunate back to front English names.

Sand flats fenced off from livestock were a glory of trefoil and other flowers enumerated for the Inishmore sands, resembling the machair of Atlantic facing coasts in the Hebrides. With them were dovesfoot and Pyrenean cranesbill, ox-eye daisies and yarrow, germander speedwell and broomrape, sorrel, dock, sea beet, three plantains and three clovers.

No better example of 'fence line ecology' could be found than that of the generously vegetated churchyard and the barrens beyond its protected boundary. The rabbit mesh and donkey proof barrier rose from a low stone wall, but severe wind scour behind this as the level outside dropped, had produced a man high sand cliff.

Outside we walked below the level of the coffins. Here it was the graves holding the ground in place rather than vice versa. Marram was still doing a good holding job on the flanks but a closed sward covered the tableland of the graveyard. The ruined church in its centre remained hidden from a little distance, having been constructed at a lower level before the major transfer of wind borne sand from the naked flats round about. The crumbling building had to be dug out at intervals to keep it visible at all. Its foundations were on a level with the oldest gravestones - more recent burials were at roof height! Gales here must send the populace scuttling indoors to avoid the desert sandstorms rather than cold air and sea spray.

The spread of sand reaching inland from the sea was laughingly referred to as the curragh factory, where the traditional island boats were made and mended or just parked until needed. Their sleek black shapes upturned on the beach put us in mind of a shoal of stranded whales. The upturned curragh progressing up the shore around the heads of the three crew-men gave the impression of an outsize bumble dor beetle, with the requisite number of six legs. These light weight boats might take off from their parking lots in a gale and were weighted down with sandbags or rocks. Those due for re-tarring were propped up on makeshift stands.

Varying in size, they resembled smaller versions of the Bering Strait Eskimos' umiaks, used for hunting seals, walrus, sea-birds and their eggs and hauling in fish on hand lines. Those wooden frames were covered with walrus hides. Aran's wooden frames were traditionally covered with cow hides, but in the twentieth century by tarred canvas. The two craft evolved independently for similar work in similar waters - a neat case of parallel evolution.

69. Lining up for the curragh race.

The light wooden frame of the curragh consists of sawn laths only 4 cm wide and 1.5 cm thick. Stouter timbers are curved to form the main ribs and the stoutest of all, about 7 x 5 cm, are used for the gunwhale. The length is 6m for a three man boat and 8m for a four man one. There is no keel, balance being maintained by rounded stones used as ballast and by the skill of the oarsmen.

Oars had no blades, unlike those of Connemara curraghs, where the ends were flattened although only slightly broadened. A triangular addition near the inner end had a hole through it to fit on the thole pin or wooden peg which served as a rowlock. This was more efficient than the usual curved metal in preventing the oar slipping overboard in a moment of crisis. Seats are narrow planks fixed near the top of the metre deep hull.

Oars were still much used and not only in the regattas, but by the seventies outboard motors often supplied the power and sometimes a small sail was hoisted, an oar over the stern serving as rudder. A rip in the fabric of the hull could be easily repaired by melting the tar round-about, putting a patch of canvas over the hole and glueing everything together with several more coats of tar.

Curraghs are used more on the smaller islands which cannot accommodate larger boats, and they are easier to pull up on the beaches. Even at Kilronan the steamer could only come in at high tide. Fishing boats of intermediate size were the wooden hulled, two masted and mechanised Galway hookers, others, rather smaller, were the new, eleven metre long lobster boats, which were more affordable for younger men starting out. A trawler in the 1970s was said to cost anything from a hundred and fifty thousand to a million pounds, depending on size.

By then the new Aran Island Fleet, based at Kilronan employed eighty five full time fishermen drawn from all the islands. It consisted of twenty one wooden hulled boats from nine metres long to nine medium sized trawlers, six larger ones and the others half decked lobster boats.

A trawl net would catch haddock, cod, plaice, sole and other bottom feeding fish and could also be usd as a drift net pulled between two boats to skim herring and mackerel from the surface waters. Catches were landed at Galway Bay for export to the continent. This entailed a five hour round trip from the home grounds, necessary also for refueling, but a more convenient port was to be developed at Rossaveal, only an hour's voyage from Inishmore on the adjacent mainland.

On moving further, our impression of Inisheer on this first short visit was of plenty of the same sort of partially bare limestone karst country as Inishmore, but the little fields seemed greener, the cattle plumper and more folk were seen at work about their houses and gardens.

The sizable iron Plassy shipwreck lay high and dry on the shore beyond An Loch Mor Lake, which huddled at the base of a low vertical cliff. A pair of mute swans sailed its waters, escorting four small cygnets, while gulls planed smoothly overhead, with querulous mewings. A sandwich tern was seen, along with ringed plover and turnstones on the beach. Little terns were dive-bombing, suggesting that they must be nesting, and an arctic tern, shouting from its perch on a post, may have been doing likewise.

70. Ringed Plovers and Sandwich Tern

Lake water was patently brackish, with scurvy grass among sea arrow-grass and Enteromorpha. The backing cliff was almost invisible under its cloak of ivy, similar but lower rock faces rising behind in a series of narrow terraces, each with its quota of parallel walls. The whole rose like a giant stairway to the scatter of white-washed houses above. Choughs were tumbling around the massive walls of another blocky prehistoric fort on the horizon. Some authorities believe these forts to be megalithic, dating from two thousand BC.

All too soon we were paddling back through the shallows to our return boat, picking shelly treasures from the translucent water. The desire to return was strong. It was as well that I did not know that the oppotunity would not come for another twenty seven years.

It was our nursing acquaintance on Inishmore who had said: "The visitors have affected us islanders and broadened our vision, but the islands affect the visitors even more deeply." For those of us who are addicted to islands anyway, these blocks of silver limestone rising from the western ocean are magic indeed!

By June 2006 Inisheer appeared on leaflets and billboards as the Irish Inis Oirr, with no cross reference to the name appearing on our maps. Translated this is 'Eastern Isle", the one nearest to the mainland. This was our hoped for target.

Today's voyage was but a short six miles from Doolin in County Clare. In the 1970s our passage to Inishmore in the freight boat with the livestock had been of twenty five miles from Galway in the next county, as the islands straddle the border. Our voyage to Inisheer the first time had been of nine miles on an open fishing boat berthed at Inishmore.

"Tranquility", our modern craft, was very different. Her under cover seats were upholstered, as in a coach, set out in twelve rows, four each side of the central gangway with four more behind - a hundred in all. It was probably as well that most passengers were continuing the extra nine miles to Cilronan. Holiday visitors to the Aran Islands in 2003 are said to have numbered two hundred and fifty thousand. The islands are closer to the mainland now not only in sea miles but in every aspect of their development.

Our party of botanists trundled down Fisher Street from Doolin in the bus that had been transporting us around the enchanted landscape of the Burren, arriving well ahead of our ten o'clock departure time.

The low promontary to seaward of the jetty was of limestone pavement, like everything else hereabouts. That it was sometimes awash with sea spray was shown by the salt marsh rush and sea plantain squeezed into crevices among the flowers of sea mayweed.

71. Sea Slater and Dwarf Sea Plantain

A large sea slater *(Ligia oceanica)* scuttled among our feet as we queued to board and was passed from hand to hand, marking our group out as oddities. Returning locals were probably too familiar with wood lice in their kitchen to get excited about the larger marine version.

A few jellyfish undulated about the prow of the waiting craft - outliers of the throng of several thousand seen the previous day stranded on the spreading sands and rocky reefs of Fanore Beach south of Black Head on the mainland. These were the common species *(Aurelia aurita)*, the gonads appearing as four mauve arcs centred around the hub of the dome. The horde had been dumped among an even larger number of tiny live periwinkles *(Littorina neritoides)* inhabiting crevices at the highest reach of the tides.

"Tranquility" pulled away from the concrete standing to skirt the northern flank of Crab Island just offshore. - heading out towards a flurry of little terns hovering close to the water, fish spotting.

Herring gulls and a pair of greater black-backs nested on Crab Island, the latter surveying us haughtily from the two highest points, but it was the black guillemots that drew the most exclamations of delight. These stood almost erect among the horizontal bodies of the cosmopolitan oyster catchers, watching the boat from low rocks in the south.

Some of their kind had entranced us the day before near Poulsallagh, just opposite. Those had returned repeatedly to a nook only just below the cliff edge but shielded from sight by a protruding ledge. After each circular flight they alighted within a few yards of the several cameras that recorded images of their dapper black and white plumage for poster-ity. Seemingly daring, they were probably aware that they were in no danger with all that empty air beyond in which to escape. I learned later that a hundred and ninety six pairs of these rare north-western auks were breeding on the Aran Islands, nine of them on Inisheer.

Redshank and purple sandpiper were spied on low shelves and rock doves are known to be present. A rock pipit volplaned out from the shore to get tossed around in the gusty wind. Soon we were headed out to sea, our attention drawn by a flock of diving gannets. Common guillemots mingled with razorbills and there were a few cormorants and fulmar petrels.

72. Cory's and Manx
Shearwaters

We were lucky to spot some large Cory's shearwaters among the scatter of home-based Manx shear-waters, these one and a half times as long in the body as the Manx (45 cm as opposed to 30 cm). Much paler, they were brownish grey where the others were black, particularly around the head and neck.

They were, indeed, the size of lesser black-backed gulls, but they 'sheared' the waves in the approved shearwater style, their sharply angled wings spanning 120 cm compared with 70 in the Manx. Their island nest sites are further south in the Mediterranean and off the Atlantic coast of Spain.

Standing on the lower stern deck comparing sizes some of us were swamped by a freak wave swirling in under the rail at deck level, triggering a partial exodus to the warmth within. When we emerged at the Inisheer pier, there were common terns diving for fish closeby.

Several other boats followed us in to the substantial quay. As these drew away a much larger, half full container boat eased her way in to unload, evidently doing the round of the islands as the old lighthouse relief boat had done in the past. Most disembarking passengers drifted towards the aroma of coffee emanating from the nearby cafe. Our return was on the much smaller, rather shabby Doolin Ferry, with a few rows of seats in the cabin, some 'park benches' amidships and standing room only on the stern deck. It was raining gently by then but no matter, we had managed a dry, if cloudy, walkabout on the island.

I was expecting changes with the burgeoning of tourism after all these years and changes there certainly were. Instead of the loose sprawl of thatched cottages, a whole little township had sprung up, with spanking new two storey houses, tiled, rendered and newly whitewashed, spreading up the slope behind. There were two pubs, a hotel, a restaurant and a shop as well as the pierhead cafe which was doing such a thriving trade.

In place of the free range donkeys nonchalently doing their own thing on the spreading sands, a small fleet of horse-drawn buggies queued to take new arrivals on a tour of the sights. Last time the tiny donkey carts had carried only locals, but we saw not a single donkey all day. Remarking on this later to a farmer, we learned that donkeys now commanded high prices and had all been sold to the mainland and converted into cash. Much of the common grazing had thus been spared, but the diesel bill for tractors and vans had increased.

The small work horses drawing the jaunting cars came in every colour pattern. Some were stockily built, their fetlocks feathered like shire's, others slighter with clean heels. Some of the vehicles they pulled were DIY versions with bench seats placed on an open cart body furnished with pneumatic tyres. There were eight such vehicles competing to take customers on a jaunt along the flat road skirting beach, air strip and elevated churchyard. Ponies walked, trotted or made occasional attempts to break into a canter before being reined back.

Upturned curraghs were scattered acrosss the sandy beach as before - affording handy windbreaks for picnic parties - but the spread of sand was greatly diminished. I had expected significant changes in the reclamation experiment after nearly thirty years and the change on the upshore flats was phenomenal. The experimental plots of 1979 were much enlarged, a far greater area being completely vegetated and fenced against livestock, although livestock seemed no longer present, at least on this day, to pose a threat.

The tentative sward of bird's foot trefoil, sea spurge and rosette plants scattered over the now more stable sand between the marram topped ridges had burgeoned into a neat grass sward. The seaward ridge had stabilised as an effective wind break tapering into a fore dune community behind the beach. It sheltered a little cluster of blue tents and the expanse of grass extended well beyond the former landward ridge as the fences had been set progressively further back.

73. "Cromlech" picnic table

The whole was now laid out as recreational parkland with circular stone enclosures planted with young trees and wind resistant shrubs such as Fuchsia. The picnic table was a giant slab of limestone laid athwart blocks at each end, like an ancient dolmen. Blocks alongside served as benches and a smaller stone edifice as a barbecue site.

The airstrip had been neatened with navy blue tarmac bordered by white markers. A well vegetated slope had built up against the further sand cliff demarcating the elevated graveyard. Part of this had been stabilised with a neat new wall protecting a concrete ramp leading up to a wrought iron gate set in the old stone archway. This and the path within would ease the task of coffin bearers, many of the graves bearing recent dates.

The little road we followed along the back of the recreation area had a newly planted hedge or shelter belt to landward, protected on either side by a mesh fence. Magenta pyramidal orchids were scattered along its base, these spilling uphill over the vegetated sand towards the buried church. With them there were a few bee orchids - often to be found in new plant successions.

Leaves of these are produced well ahead of the flowers and often become blackened from the tips down, usually from late frosts, but more likely from salt scorch here. Those of the bee orchids were black, those of the pyramidals had shrivelled to brown. Fragrant orchids seen later had escaped damage.

Lady's bedstraw snaking among their stems bore a froth of yellow flowers and there were some fine patches of squinancywort thriving on the high lime content of the sand. The little tube at the base of each flower distinguished this from similar white bedstraws and some of the clumps here were of an exquisite pale pink.

Considerable tracts were covered with short yellow rattle plants, their stems and leaves dark red, a phenomenon sometimes arising from water stress. Like the related eyebright, yellow rattle is a semi parasite, some of the lateral rootlets tapping into the roots of grasses or other plants to obtain water and minerals. Plants can survive without this help but are usually stunted. Perhaps these had failed to penetrate suitable hosts. Their presence was interesting anyway, because they are supposed to be a hallmark of ancient grassland. This area was not any sort of grassland when last viewed but just a spread of almost bare sand.

The matrix now was of sea couch, sand sedge and red fescue grass with field daisies and the all pervasive bird's foot trefoil. Red, white and alsike clovers wove among them and around upstanding cat's ear. Most persistent of the attendant butterflies were common blues and red admirals.

Some of the little erosion faces a foot or so high were clad in black moss and bordered below with lines of yellow biting stonecrop. More stable turf within a walled enclosure contained clumps of kidney vetch and hop trefoil topped by ox-eyed daisies.

Barer patches bore neat mats of rigid fern grass *(Catapodium rigidum)* and early flowering thyme-leaved sandwort among ribwort and buckshorn plantain. These communities recovering from heavy wear and tear showed none of the gems of the Inishmore dunes such as the purple Danish milk vetch.

The elevated burial site reached via the new ramp and wrought iron gate is Teampall Chaomhain, the tenth century church of St Carvan or St. Chaomhain, the patron saint of Ireland, to whom the islanders had turned in times of illness.

Here we walked at the same level as the peaks of the three arches that had supported the church roof, now missing. None of the building would be visible above ground level if it had not been periodically dug out to free it from drifting sand. The excavation had been done annually on 14th June, St. Carvan's holy day - just three days before our visit.

This annual chore was no longer necessary now that there was so much less sand on the move and with that deposited earlier now held fast by the new plant cover. Certainly there was no loose sand thrown back around the crumbling walls, as in our old photos. Nevertheless no-one had risked building their new houses on the stabilised sands with so much solid rock around.

Threading our way between the more recently erected gravestones, many in remembrance of members of the O'Donnell and Flaherty families, we were impressed at how much of the original stabilising marram grass persisted from the original dune building phase. Some had been roughly chopped back to make way for sorrel and legumes, with ox-eyed daisies conspicuous as grave ornaments.

This churchyard is in the north-east, overlooking the air strip. There is another, even older church, the ninth century Teampall or Cill Ghobnait, the church of St. Ghobnait, in the north-west. St. Ghobnait is one of the only two female saints associated with the Aran Islands and is the patron saint of bee keepers. but we saw no bee hives in our wanderings.

There was no shortage of bumble bees in places where these were not in danger of being blown out to sea. Workers of several species zoomed contentedly from flower to flower and this time we were able to examine the special Aran bee that we had sought in vain last time on Inishmore.

74. Aran Bee and Bulbous Buttercup

This was possible because our party leader, Brian Eversham from Cambridge, was an entomologist as well as a botanist. Almost confined to Aran, although seen also on the Hebrides, this is a sub-species of one of the carder bees *(Bombus muscorum* ssp. *smithianus)*, not meriting full specific status as it is at the end of a cline, the characters of the one grading gradually into the other. The type species has a narrow black and yellow band on the largely yellow abdomen, Smith's bee has no black hairs in its furry mantle.

We watched it here nectaring among the buttercups on red valerian flowers. These last are unusual in presenting their nectar at the base of the extra long and narrow spur which houses the single stamen.

Another insect of note was the transparent winged burnet moth *(Zygaena purpuralis)*, which has two continuous patches of crimson on the forewings instead of the five or six spots of the common species, and the

Skokholm

Old Red Sandstone cliffs and north-east stack. View to mainland

Bluebells near Spy Rock, lighthouse relief boat

Manx Shearwater

Skokholm Neck, view to Skomer and Middleholm

Puffins

Cape Clear 1

Pony cart meets the mail boat "Puffin"

Harbour House, Bird watchers' H Q.

Apparatus for tarring nets. New Zealand Flax left

Fishing boats in Inner Basin

Cape Clear 2

Fifteenth century church, North Harbour

*Kidney Vetch on St. Kerian's
chapel ruins*

*Skeleton of pirated wall on abandoned
farmland*

'Gate' of piled boulders across path

Cape Clear 3

The island poet and Harbour House in 1963

Vertical strata of western cliffs

O'Driscoll's Castle, used by gulls and Hooded Crows

Pond formed over old lazy beds

Cape Clear 4

Livestock by Lough Errull

Outlet from Lough Errull

Lake water tumbles over cliff

Rabbit warren in mounded Thrift, Heather beyond

Rabbit warren in herb-rich sward on mobile sand

Cape Clear 5

Mechanised ridging for potatoes

Cultivating across potato ridges

The donkey that got left out!

Cultivations on slope above goose pools

Good paddocks and poor road

Cape Clear 6

Wayside snack

Curiosity

Geese, goslings and hens

*Scurvy Grass by gull feeding ground.
Remains of rabbit, bird, fish, crab and
limpet*

The Skelligs

Author (centre) at entrance to summit beehive hut

Skellig Michael, 714 feet

Skellig Michael, the Wailing Woman Rock

Little Skellig, 445 feet and home to 32,000 Gannets

The Skelligs and Glengarrif

Gannets on Little Skellig from boat

Gannet fledglings (Photographed on Bass Rock, Scotland)

Common Seals on the way to Garinish Island, Glengarriff

Glengarriff Harbour or sea lough and the Caha Mountains

Garinish Island

Martello Tower on Garinish. View to Glengarriff Castle Hotel

Italian garden, Irish hills, Glengarriff sea lough

Italian garden conjured from Sphagnum peat and heather moor

View from central pergola

Wind tattered Holly

Magnolia and Tulips

Aran Islands 1

THE ROCKS (all Inishmore except for bottom right)

Limestone pavement with embryonic grikes

More advanced erosion into clints and grikes

An erratic of igneous rock dumped when the glacial ice melted

Beach level rock pool formed by erosion of softer 'stagshorn' coral fossil. Note transverse sectioning in centre and oblique sectioning of radiating branches at sides

Undercutting of almost horizontal beds

Ivy invading faces of limestone terraces. An Loch Mor Lake, Inisheer

Aran Islands 2
COLONISATION OF LIMESTONE (all Inishmore)

Irish Saxifrage in depressions: a natural rock garden

Spring or Vernal Sandwort

Bloody Cranesbill, most colourful of grike colonisers

Burnet Rose in grike

Roseroot in grike

Danish Milk Vetch in thin layer of sand over limestone

Aran Islands 3

FIELD AND SHORE

Stone gate, 1979, Inishmore

Metal gate, 2006, Inisheer

Drinking trough with rain catchment, 1979, Inishmore

Hay fields and new building development, 2006, Inisheer

Curragh 'workshop', incomplete tarring of one boat

Sea rods or dried kelp stalks awaiting export, 1979, Cilronan pier

Aran Islands 4

LIVESTOCK (Inishmore)

Lake cut off from the sea by sand bar

Complaint or derisive laughter at his field of stone?

Ewe with twins Gort na gApill

Farmer about to set off on his donkey

Guests to lunch!

The sixth bird watcher, near Gilbert House

Aran Islands 5

FLOWERS

Dame's Violet or Sweet Rocket

Spring Gentian

Early Purple Orchid

Parasitic Red or Thyme
Broomrape

White Early Purple Orchid

Sea Pansy on sand

Sea Aster, normally a saltmarsh plant,
growing in grike

Aran 6

EROSION AND SAND

Half buried church near Cilronan on Inishmore

Loss of sand from land not stabilised by graves, Inisheer, 1979

The same after mobile sand revegetated following livestock exclusion, 2006

New Zealand Cabbage Tree in Cilronan

Church excavated from sand burial on Inisheer, 1979, O'Brien's Castle in background

Basket making with home grown withies, Inishmore

Aran 7

Experimental plot excluding grazing in 1979. Elevated churchyard on eroding sand

The same in 2006, view seaward to new dune ridge , Inisheer

Experimental plot (left) in 1979 and new more widely spaced fences

The same in 2006. Note large number of new houses

Cheveux de frise and barren landscape from walls of Dun Aengus Fort

Dubh Chathair, the Black Fort on clifftop, showing renovated hut bases

Inishbofin and Achill

Inishbofin village and quay

Inishbofin seascape and ruin

Inishbofin patchwork of fields betwen rocky ridges

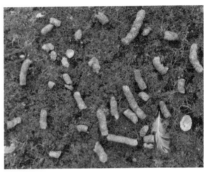

Inishbofin dung on plantain sward from wintering Barnacle Geese

Achill Island: white sand 'cowrie beach' of quartz crystals

Achill Island: slumping of peat to reveal white quartz boulders

The Isle of Man

Hawthorn blossom

Dog Rose

Wood Sorrel

Pink Purslane

European Gorse

Royal Fern

Walney Island

Cattle in Walney gullery. Piel Castle left

Lighthouse and gravel workings on south tip of bird observatory

Non-matching eggs in Lesser Black-backed Gull's nest

Creek and islet formation on eroding saltmarsh

"Nothing can find us here!"

all-over crimson of the hind wings more muted - hence the 'transparent'. We found this to be particularly common on the Burren. Being plain red rather than spotted, it was more likely to be confused with the cinnabar moth than the locally common six spot burnet.

75. *Transparent and Six Spot Burnet Moths*

A beetle coming to notice was *Dascillus cervinus*, falling midway between the soldier beetles and the click beetles. It is the only species in its family, a dusky pale brown and rather bigger than the abundant shiny bronze and green garden chafers (*Phyllopertha horticola*) which were scurrying everywhere.

Inisheer is the smallest of the three main Aran Islands, occupying 1,400 acres as opposed to 7,635 acres on Inishmore. The limestone terraces rise in a spectacular series from beach level to O'Brien's two storey castle, its square bulk dominating the island's highest point on the uppermost terrace.

This Lower Carboniferous Limestone, laid down 325 to 350 million years ago, is intercalated with harder beds of non porous shale, which hold up the water. As the porous limestone gradually erodes away with the years, the shale beds outlast them, forming the horizontal surfaces between the limestone faces, and channelling the water which has seeped down thus far onto the next shelf - often to be used as the water supply for local cottagers.

Scarp faces on Inishmore range from ten to sixteen feet high, mostly a little less on Inisheer. They are steepest and narrowest in the north and, as we ascended the lane leading to the summit, some of the grassy strips on the flat surfaces served as nothing more than footways between the narrow walled fields above and below. Many of the sheer faces were softened by thick curtains of ivy.

At the lower levels there were cottages, their walled gardens full of flowers and hardy shrubs, with Escallonia well to the fore. Dames violet (*Hesperis matronalis*) was a favourite herb - tall, elegant and with white or mauve flowers. Sweet rocket is an alternative name and a better one, for this is no shy violet but an upstanding cress which we observed romping along leafy roadsides on less open parts of the Burren. Its 'ladylike' charms were being patronised by red admirals, but the 'dames' refers to Damascus, not ladies.

77. O'Brien's Castle

Other outstanding specimens were big, mop-topped onions known as wild leeks. These were Babingtons leeks *(Allium babingtonii* or *Allium ampeloprasum* var *babingtonii)*, a seaside species found on Aran and Connemara, North-west Ireland and the tip of Cornwall, but not elsewhere. The type species of *Allium ampeloprasum* is also uncommon and in Wales is the signature species of Flatholm Island just off Cardiff although occurring rarely also in North Wales, South England and West Ireland.

Nestled in the complex of closely juxtaposed walls around O'Brien's Castle was a fine elder bush covered with flowers and in no way mis-shaped by the wind, like most. The only ornamentation on the plain, angular building were two corbels carved with human faces. It had been erected during the fourteenth or fifteenth century within the bounding walls of one of the old prehistoric forts, only one of whose walls still stands. This is Dun Formna, the fort of the ridge or hilltop, and the first stronghold to occupy this commanding position offering views over the whole island. It is less massive than most and thought to have been built in the Bronze Age or even earlier.

The lane we followed wound on at this level, offering superb views across the crowded fields. Smart new white houses were scattered throughout, each farmhouse close to the land which its inmates farmed. On Inishmore we remembered the cottages gathered together into social groupings, the clachans or villages, entailing longer walks, or donkey rides, to reach the fields - and sometimes to carry water during dry spells. Thus aggregated they afford each other mutual shelter from the elements.

There were fourteen villages in all there and Gort na gCapall, the field of the horses, where we had taken tea with the much travelled nurse, was the only one on the broader terraces of the low neck of land joining the two halves of the island. These were more exposed to September gales, which can reach force ten or eleven on the Beaufort scale, but the little paddocks we saw were as green as any and supported some fine fat ewes with twin lambs.

In 1640 a tidal wave had swept right across this low lying terrain, coinciding with an earthquake on the north-west coast of Europe. This might thus have been a tsunami, engendered by the earth tremor.

Roads and their walls were serviced by the locals as common property. Population at the beginning of the new millennium was approximately three hundred on Inisheer's four square miles and nine hundred on Inishmore, which is 8.5 x 2 miles.

We saw no thatched cottages at all this time, all the shining white houses being tiled with smooth slates, a darker colour than the beautifully figured Liscannor Slates which form fences around the Cliffs of Moher and non-slip pavements in the mainland town of Lisdoonvarna where we were staying.

Arable land as such seemed to be absent, now that rye straw was no longer needed for thatch and there were few or no donkeys to be fed in winter. Apparently there were still cattle about, although we saw none. Perhaps they were being kept in the old cottages now serving as barns, until the hay was cut and they could come out to crop the aftermath.

Haymaking was in full swing, grass growth often dense and mixed with plenty of tall herbs to add flavour and a variety of minerals to the mix. Quite a few of these belonged to the cow parsley family, including the greeny-yellow, essentially maritime Alexanders, some of its leaves affected by an orange rust. Here too were buttercups, yarrow and ox-eyed daisies, hawkweeds and other Composites, with Yorkshire fog grass. A particularly attractive hayfield flower was the tall cat's valerian with pale pink flowers. Few of the fields were what agriculturalists would regard as improved pasture, with little else but perennial ryegrass, cocksfoot and clovers.

The crop was harvested with hand tools, the swathes left as they fell, not raked into rows nor tossed to dry with a swathe turner. We saw no-one working in the fields, perhaps because it was Saturday, but the hay harvest, standing or cut, was reasonably thick and nowhere on our walk down the island's eastern flank did we see the expanses of bare, uncultivable limestone pavement so prevalent on Inishmore twenty seven years before. Covering the rocky bones of the land with sand and seaweed was much simpler now that tractors and trailers had replaced donkeys and man power.

At intervals we had to squeeze ourselves back against the lane walls to allow a heavy tractor to trundle past, but there were few fields with gates big enough to let this mechanical monster through and few large enough to make the effort worth while. Turning at the headlands would entail enough continuous circuits to induce giddiness if entry was attained.

Gates were being updated, however, and we saw far fewer consisting of piled stones between the sturdy gateposts. Many were now of tubular steel, mostly footpath sized, but a few bigger ones. Some of the more sophisticated were fixed to breeze block gateposts instead of limestone slabs or, if of piled blocks, these cemented for ease of securing the gate hinges.

And then there were 'intermediate' style gates of discarded wooden palettes or rusty oil drums pending the acquisition of something more easily managed. As on the mainland, the field sized metal gates were six barred instead of five barred like traditional wooden ones. Most were fastened with wooden pegs or binder twine.

There seemed to be fewer water troughs on this island, but all those seen now had cement facing on the walls as well as the catchment slope. One was noticed with a metal sheet for catchment and the trough lidded, the field served being currently under a hay crop. But, where were the farm animals? As stated, we saw neither donkeys nor cows, no goats, pigs or poultry, only one horse out of harness and one lone sheep. This was a solitary ram in a tiny paddock with a ten inch enamel bowl, now empty, lodged against a tussock.

A few small plots had been planted with potatoes, now at peak of flowering. Others bore fully blown cabbages, smaller Brassicas, onions and frilly modern, purple or green lettuce varieties. No cereals or soft fruits were seen, just the odd abandoned car or piled organic matter.

When the others turned back for a cafe lunch and visit to the craft shop I pressed on towards the south-eastern lighthouse. Floral garlands along the lane verges were a constant delight, ranging from upstanding tree mallow to ground level field mouse-ear *(Cerastium arvense)*. Both grew alongside more familiar relatives, common mallow and snow-in-summer *(Cerastium tomentosum)*, an aggressive creeper likely to be a garden escape.

Shining cranesbill with its highly polished leaves and inflated, lantern-like calyces, grew in wall crannies. The larger flowered Pyrenean or hedgerow cranesbill and two-flowered or long-stalked cranesbill mingled with the ubiqui-

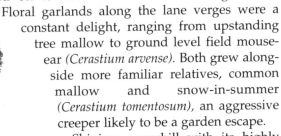

78. Babington's Leek

tous herb Robert along their bases. Poppies, speedwell and many more survived the attentions of the army of snails - *Helix aspersa* and *Cepaea nemoralis.*

A robust clump of bush vetch rooted high on a wall came cascading down in atypical profusion towards some delicate white ramping fumitory *(Fumaria capreolata)*. Bulbous buttercup, silverweed, heath violet and wood sage added their quota of colour at ground level and pellitory-of-the-wall was very much at home on the wealth of vertical faces.

Some of these were thickly beset with ivy, excluding all else except the occasional, billious looking spike of parasitic ivy broomrape. Dense curtains of this pernicious but ecologically friendly creeper clothed the limestone faces around a deep water filled hollow supporting tall willows which proved to be hybrids between osiers and goat sallow *(Salix viminalis X caprea)*. A passing local intimated that this was a bottomless pit. "Fall in there and ye're dead!"

Appropriately the commonest butterflies were the prettily patterned wall butterflies basking on walls, as so often, but with no sunshine to bask in today. I ate my frugal repast of biscuits and apple comfortably perched on one of the flat horizontal stones protruding from a wall face as step-over stiles, leaning back against the wall watching them.

I had turned off the lane along which the tractor rumbled at intervals, onto a side track where bird life was less disturbed. The two red-billed choughs passing overhead, with their lilting, bleating calls, like high pitched versions of effeminate jackdaws, were visible from everywhere, I learned later that some five pairs of choughs breed on Inisheer, along with hooded crows and jackdaws, but, understandably, with no arable land there were no rooks.

A diminutive wren foraged jauntily along the wall base until it happened upon the bonanza of an army of bustling ants. These kept it busy for a while. The inevitable robin trilled its little song from a bramble-draped gatepost. Distant cuckoo calls had intruded on the constant twitter of swallows all morning at intervals, a sound evocative of childhood years but seldom heard on the mainland these days.

My chief serenaders were members of a little possie of linnets moving restlessly back and forth between walltop and thorn scrub entwined with honeysuckle. These apparently replace the absent chaffinches and green-finches and the only other finches we saw were goldfinches at nut feeders back in the northern gardens, where they were in competition with the more numerous house sparrows and starlings.

Peering over a high wall to a much used paddock generously laced with aromatic piles of horse dung and burgeoning bramble patches, I spotted a dunnock and a couple of blackbirds exploiting the enhanced fertility. A stonechat appeared briefly on a sprig of unripe rose hips.

Stinging nettles were crowded on worn patches where the equines had stood head to tail in bouts of mutual preening and fly swatting. Some of the coprophiles were decorated with smooth, white pimple galls on the leaf backs and stalks and at the base of axillary shoots. Causers were midges, the nettle gnats *(Dasynura urticae)*. A single egg is laid in May to produce each gall, this darkening as it matures for the larva to emerge in autumn and pupate in the ground. New adults break free in spring to repeat the cycle.

Reddening spikes of wild Arum berries around this field margin may have indicated a former tree or scrub cover, represented now by spiky sloe bushes and romping honeysuckle. Primroses, ramsons or broad-leaved garlic, hemp agrimony and certain ferns are other woodland understorey plants occurring.

As I pressed on to the lighthouse a skylark trilled ecstatically, headed into the wind but making no progress during its repeated song flights. The country opened out here, with progressively more limestone slabs pushing through the grass cover. This was where the wheatears and meadow pipits came into their own.

Wood pigeons of the more crowded landscape to the north had faded from the scene and I saw instead a couple of rock doves, recognisable by their white rumps, the two black bars on the pale upper wing and narrow black border on the white underwing. These are the ancestors of the familiar feral pigeons of our cities, which have evolved endless variations of plumage pattern. Some retain the ancestral garb and their lineage is always suspect if not in such places as this where there are ample cliff crevices for them to set up home as their forebears did.

It is suspected that the famous dovecote of Culver Hole on the Gower coast in South Wales was constructed to entice some of the plentiful, cliff nesting rock doves into niches from which they could be more conveniently exploited for winter rations. This, like Aran, is of Carboniferous Limestone, the elongated cleft thought to have been walled off with limestone blocks around 1353 *(Alfred Watkins, 1891. Archeological Society Journal, 48.)*. Culver is the old English name for pigeon, so this may have signalled the beginning of their domestication and invasion of our parks and gardens and railway stations countrywide.

The predominantly white lighthouse with broad black band amidships and narrower one at the base, tapered elegantly skyward to the narrower lantern chamber atop. The landward side of the latter was blocked to shield the scattered dwellings from the flashing that warned mariners away.

It was automated now, like all the rest, but the two neat light-keepers' cottages were still intact on its western side, their slate roofs shining silver in the reflected light from the sea. When manned, until 1978, the keepers here at Poinnte an Fhardarus light worked one month on duty and enjoyed one month off with their families. I looked in vain for porpoises or dolphins beyond their lonely outpost, the fins of any present lost among the turbulence of white horses.

6

Inishbofin, Connemara and Achill Island, Co. Mayo

MOORLAND WILD AND TAMED

Inishbofin lies twelve miles north west of Clifden off the Connemara coast. Deeply embayed in the north and east and with its capacious harbour in the south, it is three miles from east to west and some two miles from north to south. It is served by the mail boat from Cleggan, seven miles away and a once important fishing port, for both commercial catches and deep sea angling trips.

The name Bofin Island equates with the Island of the White Cow, though the cattle seen were all black or skewbald. Inishturk away to the north, equates with Boar Island, but has no wild boars and apparently never has had.

Like so many other Celtic Isles, Bofin was selected as a retreat by holy men and St. Colman founded a monastery here in the seventh century. In 1652 it surrendered to the Cromwellians and remained a Roundhead garrison until 1700. It is reputed to have served as a sort of concentration camp for monks and priests, and Cromwell's barracks stood menacingly at the harbour entrance through ensuing centuries as a reminder.

Our party visited in mid July, 1970, finding a friendly welcome in the accommodating natural harbour, with its two hotels and clustered cottages. The backdrop stretching away across the slightly sloping plain was of well tended fields - larger and greener than those fashioned by the Aran Islanders and all neatly rectangular, uninterrupted by the knolls and outcrops that eliminate the possibility of mechanisation on Aran. This landscape is not webbed with criss crossing walls and might look like an Aran Islander's dream.

Not so! All seemed hunky dory for a comfortable island life compared with the hardships endured on Aran, but we were there in midsummer. As on all the rest, life was very different when winter gales roared across the bleak moorland and Atlantic rollers battered the ancient cliffs.

Many Inishbofin islanders escaped to the mainland in winter and - fourteen years later - the entire island was abandoned by all except a trio of die-hards who remained stubbornly put. While the Aran islanders

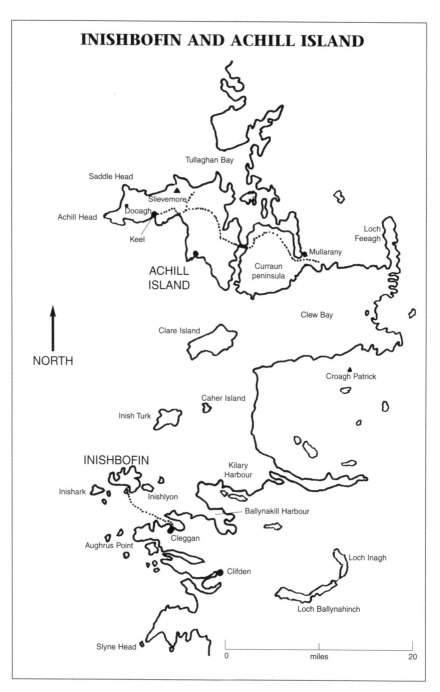

INISHBOFIN AND ACHILL ISLAND

Tullaghan Bay

Saddle Head

Slievemore

Dooagh

Achill Head

Keel

ACHILL
ISLAND

Curraun
peninsula

Mullarany

Loch
Feeagh

NORTH

Clew Bay

Clare Island

Croagh Patrick

Caher Island

Inish Turk

INISHBOFIN

Kilary
Harbour

Inishark

Inishlyon

Ballynakill Harbour

Aughrus Point

Cleggan

Loch Inagh

Clifden

Loch Ballynahinch

Slyne Head

0   miles   20

were moving into an age of comparative prosperity, the Bofin islanders opted out, at least until better times to come.

"The Observer" newspaper of 25th November 1984 reported the general exodus as an epitaph to the death of a community. After five hundred years of hauling half their living from the sea and scratching the other half from the land, the population was moving out. The same had happened on the Great Blasket off the Dingle Peninsula - the vacated acres abandoned to rabbits, sheep, and sea-birds.

From a hundred and twenty eight persons in 1968, two years before our visit, the Inishbofin population dwindled steadily. The death knell was sounded when the postmistress closed the post office and decamped with her husband and four teen age children, six years after the school had closed. It was the fear of being unable to obtain help in the case of emergency that finally triggered the exodus for all but the few.

Hannah McFaddon, an independent matron in her fifties, was satisfied with her meagre lot and elected to stay where she had been brought up. I quote:-

"I think it's the best place in the world. I've lost my temper and I've lost my nerve sometimes, but I've never lost my faith. Everyone will be back. As far as I'm concerned, they haven't left. On the mainland there's drinking and fighting and quarrelling. I listen to the radio and there's disasters everywhere. As long as I'm safe in this house and have enough supplies, I'll stay."

Spinach, kale, cabbages, brussel sprouts and tomatoes sprouted defiantly from peaty garden soil where a few hens scratched and no Irish small holder is without a cache of potatoes. A solitary cow, a couple of dogs, a sister also opting to stay and a bowl of carragheen soaking to accompany the breakfast egg. What more could a body want?

With hindsight, in these days of helicopters and daily air-sea-rescue exploits around the coast, she may well have been proved right about the return of her fellow islanders. With two hotels and delightfully indented bays and beaches, this could be a summer paradise for tourism, attracting some of the many who come to enjoy the famous twelve Bens of Connemara and the delights of Ballinakill and Killary Harbours on the adjacent mainland.

But in 1984 Inishbofin still had no roads, no deep water harbour, no mains electricity, no shop, no school and no post office.

"All we want is a telephone service and a helicopter service" said a spokesman for the eight man island council in that fateful year. There seems little reason why these amenities that most of us take for granted should not have been installed by now to tempt some brave souls back.

The day fixed for our visit to Inishbofin proved too rough to attempt the crossing. The sea was a grey and white violence, the breakers curling shorewards with a minty blue glint. We proceeded instead to Lough Renvyle on the mainland immediately opposite. Only a bank of churning pebbles separated this from an almost landlocked embayment of the sea, with bubbly blobs of spume sailing in over the bluff beyond, each on a little cushion of air.

The none too fresh corpse of a dolphin had been cast up on the confining beach, a source of interest to a scavenging herring gull. Thirty five ringed plovers pottered unconcernedly round about. Although having such distinctively patterned black and white plumage, these merged imperceptibly, in perfect harmony with the mottled background of highlights and shadows. But those pebbles formed an effective barrier to the sea and there was no hint of brackishness in the lake water behind.

Small sand deposits on the beach crest harboured rabbits and it was here that we sought the rare variant Irish form of hairy rock cress (*Arabis hirsuta v. brownii*), but without success. We did, however, come upon the little flat pom-pom flower heads of pipewort (*Eriocaulon aquaticum*), rising from rigid rosettes

79. *Pipewort, Perfoliate Pondweed and Nuttall's Waterweed*

of translucent leaves in shallow water. This unglamorous but unmistakable rarity characterises soggy peat on the western peninsulas of Ireland but is rare in similar locations in Scotland and not to be expected at all in England or Wales.

Local botansists had asked us to keep a lookout for Hydrilla, an exceedingly scarce waterweed suspected to be here, although modern texts report it as only on "One lough in Western Ireland and one loch in South Scotland", the Irish one not far from here. Our suspected candidate for this honour was flowering and turned out to be nuttall's pondweed (*Elodea nutallii*), a narrow-leaved version of the ubiquitous invasive Canadian pondweed.

There was much more to keep us busy around this water lily lake, not least St. Patrick's cabbage with ragged robin, purple loosestrife and water mint. An unusual relative of the broad-leaved pondweed, with its gradation from linear submerged leaves to broad floating ones, was the perfoliate pondweed, with elegantly transparent underwater foliage, its broad bases clasping the stems.

Back in Clifden we retired to the noisy babble of roosting jackdaws and woke to the distraut lowing of displaced cattle - this being market day and the streets rippling with beasts driven in from the hills. Extricating ourselves from the melée, we boarded our transport to Cleggan, our port of embarkation.

We were not travelling on the normal pasenger boat, having booked a cheaper one kept on the island, through Mrs. Day, proprietor of one of the two island hotels. (Ten shillings each instead of eighteen shillings in those thrifty days of the twenty shilling pound.) This was a working boat with minimal seating but the sea was calm, the rain had stopped and the hour's crossing was full of interest.

Gannets and guillemots skimming the open sea were replaced by greater black-backed and herring gulls as we drew into the haven, with Inishlyon to starboard and Inishark to port. Alongside the jetty was a stony beach grading to a sandier top with a succulent sea sandwort sward. Sea mayweed, sea radish, cleavers and much more helped to hold the pebbles together.

Only the Lewissian Gneiss is older than the ancient core of Inishbofin. The island's pre-Cambrian, Dalradian rocks rise, impregnably hard, as a series of low hillocks. Inishturk, the next sea girt outcrop of similar size to the north, is much newer geologically, being of Ordovician age.

Inishturk's strata form alternate ribs and furrows, the terrain showing a greater diversity of wild flowers in relation to its size (of two and a quarter square miles) than the larger Inishbofin. It includes some splendid cliffs in the west.

Inishbofin is flatter. The windshorn heather moor is dotted with small lakes and bog pools as well as the considerable acreage of grass fields, while the little sandy bays are a delight. Everywhere were intrusive rock outcrops, like the bones of an emaciated horse showing through the taut, dun skin. Only in the wet hollows did the soil cover seem much more than rudimentary. The ice age had left the bedrock scoured and barren and we could only wonder how many more rock layers had built up on the ancient Dalradian surface and been worn away again before the ice moved in to do its worst.

A stony track led up from the pier through a cluster of buildings to the knobbly moorland above. The parent rock thrusting up through the superficial skin of heather incorporated shining white patches of quartz. These were unusually extensive, appearing as sheets or veins insinuated through the darker matrix. Predominantly siliceous, they added fewer beneficial minerals to the soil than do the shining white calcites of the Aran limestone.

Uncompromising tufts of black bog rush *(Schoenus nigricans)* poked up through the ling even in quite salty situations, along with more splayed tufts of wiry deer-grass *(Trichophorum caespitosum)*, this a sedge, not a grass. True sedges included star, yellow, oval and carnation *(Carex echinata, C. demissa, C. ovalis* and *C. flacca)* .

Among unruly tussocks of purple moor grass was the smaller bobble-fruited heath grass which has recently sacrificed its entity as *Sieglingia decumbens* to become afiliated with the Australian Danthonias as *Danthonia decumbens.* More special was the viviparous form of fescue grass *(Festuca vivipara)* with leafy tufts sprouting in lieu of flower heads.

80. Deer Grass, Black Bog Rush and Viviparous Fescue

Damper spots were enhanced by the fragile pink of bog pimpernel, lesser skullcap and lousewort and more sombre mauves of devil's bit scabious, sheeps bit and marsh violet with its more than usually round leaves and flowers.

81. *Spotted Rock Rose and Yellow Bartsia*

Drier ridges might be crowned with low mats of gorse with spikes of medieval ferocity. The brilliance of their well protected blooms was augmented by the more modest but ubiquitous tormentil and rare, red-splotched spotted rock-rose *(Tuberaria guttata)*. This grows also among the heather of South Stack on the Welsh island of Anglesey but almost nowhere else in Great Britain and Ireland, except County Cork in the South-west. Yellow bartsia

141

(*Parentucellia viscosa*) is another rarity here - an essentially maritime plant of southern and western coasts.

The skin of turf over the unwelcoming rock dwindles to nothing at its seaward limits. It yields a poor, fibrous peat, which burns more wastefully than the chocolate slabs of well matured sods. The slane or turf cutter with the two blades joined at right angles is unable to cut it out in neat oblongs for stacking in little wigwams, the uneven slices, often with twiggy inclusions, being piled in untidy heaps to await collection.

Fine-leaved heath mingled with the ling throughout, while cross-leaved heath took over around the beer coloured pools of peaty water. At Roundstone a few miles from Clifden, we had come across Mackay's heath *(Erica mackaiana),* found only in this north-west corner of Ireland, but this produces its fine pink flower bells later in the summer, so we failed to spot it on the island. It can hybridise with the cosmopolitan cross-leaved heath so might be in danger of losing its specific identity. Another of this ilk at Roundstone and a Connemara speciality is St. Dabeoc's heath *(Daboecia cantabrica),* with a slender head of more widely spaced pink bells.

82. St.Dabeoc's Heath and Mackay's Heath

Blechnum hard fern rosettes were tucked among the Inishbofin heathers and noble plants of royal fern found a living in the lee of sheltering knolls. At the other extreme there was nothing but lichens, principally Cladonias and Parmelias, clothing the ground. Elsewhere were dark shaggy tufts of Britain's tallest moss, *Polytrichum commune,* along with lighter patches of *Leucobryum glaucum* and *Rhytidiadelphus aureus.*

The new green pastures cut from that dark moorland had had to be worked for, but by breaking down the soil rather than building it up as on Aran. Here the fibrous turf was skimmed off and drainage runnels dug to allow air into formally sodden peat so that micro-organisms could digest the unrotted plant remains and release such few nutrients as they contained. This was a very different approach from the sand and seaweed recipe on Aran's more kindly limestone, and not necessarily any easier to achieve. Inishbofin had too much organic and too little mineral material; Aran had too few 'organics' to mitigate a superfluity of minerals.

Greatest diversity was to be found in depressions where water collected to afford unwilling nourishment to bog plants. Mysteriously dark yet clear pools mirrored the sky, providing nurseries for dragonflies and damselflies, water boatmen and pond skaters. Much was just an overall quagmire, where water and plant matter were inextricably mixed. Gentle pressure caused the vegetation to sink into the tawny fluid, disturbing the aquatic larvae of midges and other bird food. Here was the usual cycle of birth and death, but lacking the expected corollary of decay, so that the dead lingered on, to build up the level over the centuries.

Most of the slender store of nutrients is leached away in the slightly acidic rain water - sideways in runnels or downward to levels too poor in oxygen to harbour plant roots. Sunlight nurtures a surface film of aquatic algae and this provides a substrate for the first more substantial incomers, the Sphagnum mosses.

To obtain sufficient nutrients from the almost pure rain water these are furnished with a series of large empty cells, allowing them to imbibe and store a more than normal amount of water. Each mini reservoir is surrounded by narrower green cells carrying out the vital photosynthesis. This water holding sponge was exploited by medical crews in wartime, the honeycomb being used as an absorbent. In the hills behind Aberystwyth in West Wales streams polluted with heavy metals from mining operations could be cleansed by diverting them through absorbent Sphagnum beds.

The moss produces hydrogen ions which can be swapped for other minerals essential for its own growth, the mine water thus able to pass unwanted metallic elements to the motley of different Sphagnum species. These mosses can form a mosaic of different colours in space or a succession in time - yellow species invading the deeper water and being gradually overtaken by others of different hues, from pea green to cranberry red.

Every bog walker knows how treacherous these bog communities can prove, but they gradually solidify, excluding the entry of atmospheric oxygen and inhibiting proliferation of the aerobic (oxygen demanding) micro-organisms responsible for breaking down the plant remains. The result is an accumulating mass of undecayed vegetable matter, often composed principally of Sphagnum, instead of the more usual humus-rich, earthworm-friendly growing medium.

Small quantities of anaerobic bog bacteria can exist, by extracting oxygen from sulphuric acid in the bog water, leaving only the hydrogen and the sulphur, combined as hydrogen sulphide - the source of that inimitable smell of rotten eggs that sometimes pervades stretches of bogland.

Unusual habitats produce unusual plants and we found an interesting range of the unusual in Inishbofin's bogs - not least the insect devouring sundews with their dewdrop spangled tentacles and butterwort, with gland-dotted rosettes of incurling leaves. Most of the swansdown of bog cotton was from the narrow-leaved, many-headed *Eriophorum angustifolium*. Commonest of the floating weeds was the bog pondweed

83. Narrow-leaved Bog Cotton and Bog Asphodel

Potamogeton polygonifolius.

With them were patches of the unwettable shoots of marsh St. John's-wort and daisy-headed sneezewort *(Achillea ptarmica)*. Most striking later on would be the yellow flower spikes of bog asphodel *(Narthecium ossifragum)*. Red-stemmed creeping water purslane *(Peplis portula)* penetrated pools of open water, sometimes with the maritime mud crowfoot *(Ranunculus baudotii)*, nudging up to swards of the more widespread marsh pennywort. Depauperate woody plants were mostly willows. Tucked away from these specialists and the impoversihed swards of mat grass *(Nardus stricta)* and fescue were more homely species such as primrose and honeysuckle.

Sea plantain swards terminating in a thin skin of turf over coastal rocks were littered with fibrous cylinders of the dried dung of the barnacle geese which come here in winter to escape the rigours of their northern breeding grounds. None of the bog or moorland communities of the rest seemed to attract these voracious grazers.

The anomalously small but still succulent plantain leaf rosettes formed a smooth green turf, closely nibbled by sheep and rabbits as well as geese, so that all available 'bite' was young. Often the diminutive flower spikes were only an inch high. this applying also to the accompanying buck's-horn and ribwort plantains and trefoils. Their dwarfness ensured the survival of species unable to attain more than a couple of inches or so in any habitat and hence squeezed out from most sites. Notable here were allseed and water blinks *(Radiola linoides* and *Montia verna)*.

Only barnacle geese winter here, grey lags and white-fronts are not attracted. Barnacles are also abundant on the neighbouring Inishturk, increasing there since that island was evacuated.

Currently, in the 1970s, the Inishbofin geese shared their gathering grounds on the island with herring and greater black-backed gulls, which coughed up crop pellets and littered the sward with pieces of crab, mussel and limpet shells, rabbit bones and other debris, some conceivably brought by the shore-feeding oyster catchers.

84. Barnacle Geese on sward of dwarf Sea Plantain

Curlews were seen resting, the disembodied calls of others wafting over the moorland. Meadow pipits and wheatears were frequent - at least when the geese were not padding around disturbing the soil fauna with their big flat feet.

All the areas in question would receive considerable douching by sea water in rough weather, inhibiting the acid-loving bog plants and twiggy heather. Similar sea plantain swards clothe cliff edges of Fair Isle and other Scottish islands, their counterpart in the less cold, less rainy seabird colonies of Wales being swards of buck's-horn plantain, with or without sea storksbill, these not attracting migratory geese.

Ornithologist Ken Williamson has observed barnacle geese grazing sea plantain on St. Kilda - and with them resting ruffs, black-tailed godwits, ringed plovers and dunlin. The taller more succulent foliage of sea plantain in its better known environment of salt marshes is a favourite food of mute swans and domesticated geese.

Clare Island, five miles north of Inishturk and ten miles north of Inishbofin, covers a little over six square miles. Its ancient dark red slates and sandstones of Dalradian age are confined to the north. Younger sandstones, shales and conglomerates of Silurian age occur in the south, separated by a major fault line and covered by layers of glacial till and peat.

ACHILL ISLAND

Achill Island, another five miles to the north, is Eagle Island, named after the white-tailed sea eagles *(Aquila albicilla)*. These noble birds were recorded by Edward Newman as being abundant here in 1838 but, by 1898, they had disappeared, leaving only a few itinerant golden eagles.

The successful reintroduction of white tailed sea eagles to some of the West Scottish Islands in recent years holds out hope that some may find

85. White-tailed Eagles

their way back to their old Irish haunts, with or without human assistance.

The modern Achill is an island only in name, the narrow arm of the sea cutting it off from Curraun being spanned by a substantial bridge. It was not until 1979 that I crossed this bridge after exploring the mussell growing project of Killary Harbour. These bivalves were being farmed on rafts anchored offshore in the sea lough.

New yellow ropes with short cross bars provided a settlement area for the free-swimming planktonic larval phase. The ropes dangled from wooden laths mounted across tubular metal floats. The infant mussels attached themselves with 'guy lines' of byssus threads, mostly in May and June, and were harvested some eighteen months later, from October to February.

Produce was exported to France, where potential mussel farmers suffered from water pollution, this not a problem in the clear seas off Western Ireland. Seed mussels two months old were being taken on their ropes to establish a new population further south in Connemara when we were there.

86. Mussel rafts

Atlantic seals basking alongside the shellfish rafts were regarded as no hazard. They were interested in bigger game and more likely to be looked on with disfavour by the men involved in the local salmon and sea trout fisheries.

Starfish and jellyfish were said to be the main predators. Evidently their dangling isolation offshore saved these mussels from ambulatory dog whelks, which drill into the shells of rock-bound mussells to savour the contents.

En route north we found yet another of the special Irish heathers. This was the Irish heath *(Erica erigena)*, the tallest of them all and half way to

146

the potential of the southern tree heath. Flowers were fully out on the five foot high bushes, pink bells with protruding purple stamens. Plants were modelled on a larger version of the common ling, but with a one-sided flower spike.

Achill Island is credited with being the most westerly part of Europe, but its island status strictly disqualifies it from this honour, which it would need to share with Inishbofin - and far distant St. Kilda - if islands were included.

The two Irish islands are composed of similar ancient rocks, the Dalradian schists and quartzites here highly folded and faulted, the terrain nearly always mountainous where the resistant quartzites appear. Achill is dominated by two towering peaks, Slievemore reaching 2,204 feet in the north and Croaghorn 2,192 feet in the west.

The extremity of Achill Island is composed of a steeply dipping layer of schist creating the knife edge ridge of Achill Head pushing out into the Atlantic. Its outstanding feature is the north-west facing cliff which plunges almost vertically from the summit cairn in a stunning precipice. These phenomena have been accorded the accolade of qualifying as some of the finest cliff scenery in Western Europe, but sadly they can be viewed to advantage only from the sea, or by the very athletic from Achill Head.

The west-facing coast of the southern peninsula leading to Keel Strand is a ridge of quartzite exposed to the full force of Atlantic breakers. It has been eroded into arches and stacks and the Cathedral Rocks, to form one of the Island's most popular tourist attractions.

Quartzites, as well as producing the most spectacular cliffscapes, are also responsible for the most sheltered beaches, the crystals released from sea battered rocks accumulating as pale sand in sheltered bays. This is siliceous, its only input of lime being from stranded sea shells, so it cannot support the lime-loving flora of Aran's more extensive sandscapes.

Hummocks of glacial drift in Eastern Achill represent the western limit of advance of Ireland's last great ice sheet - not that there was much landscape further west for it to influence. The peninsula west of Keel is of smooth hillsides sloping gently to the sea.

The two mountains over two thousand feet are thought to have been sufficiently high to have escaped ice cover as nunataks. We will never know if any pre ice age plant life survived those frozen centuries on their ice-free summits.

Beyond the edge of the main island ice sheet during the midland general glaciation, small glaciers were at work scouring out some fine corries, each with a sparkling lake impounded behind a crescentic moraine. These have been referred to by glaciologists as "A collection of glacial phenomena unequalled in the British Isles". They are to be viewed only by intrepid mountain walkers, which did not include us.

One lough is held back by its moraine on the very edge of a stupendous sea cliff. Recession of this cliff by erosion is gradually undermining the moraine so that the level of the lake is falling, leaving an abandoned shoreline. A lower lying one has the base of the moraine being actively attacked by waves. It is only a matter of time before the sea breaks through and releases the lake water, to swirl into its basin, the rock floor of which is thought to be below sea level.

Robert Lloyd-Praeger, who visited in 1898 and 1904, gives a glowing account of Achill Island in his famous book "The Way That I Went", republished by Penguin in 1969, sixteen years after his death. He speaks of "Windswept, barren peat, with great gaunt brown mountains and a wild coast hammered by Atlantic waves." The population was far larger then than the meagre agriculture and spasmodic fishing could support and was maintained on American money sent home by absent sons and daughters. Housing conditions were very bad.

The island, roadless in his day, had miles of smooth tarmac by 1979 - carrying us round the "Atlantic Drive" of the Southern Peninsula and the even nobler scenery of the west. Praeger's "savage coastline" had been invaded by caravans, housing had improved beyond recognition and there were hotels and gift shops. Achill may well have benefited further by the general uplift in living conditions after Eire joined the European Union and impoverished, sometime flea-ridden farms were converted into admirable farmhouse accommodation for discerning tourists.

The penetrating westerlies took the edge off the sunshine, which shone so much more warmly on the mainland. We lunched in the lee of a dark peat cliff, gazing out to the stark black outline of Clare Island to the south, across an unusually mirror-calm sea.

There was a clatter of hoofs as a high spirited dog chased a flock of sheep down to the seaweedy rocks, with the farmer in hot pursuit. The quarry entered the sea, with no hesitation. Buoyed up by the air in their fleeces, they swam along to an easy way up the cliff with such aplomb that we felt this was not the first time. Man and dog turned to make the rendezvous elsewhere.

As the kerfuffle subsided two mergansers flew in to spend the next half hour fishing. These are sleek, underwater swimmers like the closely related goosanders that were moving south to colonise Welsh rivers during the last years of the millennium. Nearby a sandwich tern was plunging its yellow-tipped black bill into the water as it dipped in flight for surface fish. Razorbills stayed well offshore: the swifts, sand martins and kestrel that entertained us remained airborne.

Scattered over the fine siliceous sand were ribbed cowries, edible periwinkles, three species of top shells and saddle oysters carrying adherent barnacles. Few of the sea urchin tests had washed up undamaged and the displaced limpet shells were broad and low or narrow and peaked - depending on the degree of wave action they had had to withstand when clinging to the rocks with a muscle power evolved to thwart predatory gulls and oyster catchers as well as the pull of the waves.

The mantle of heather stretched away in all directions, thinning on wind-lashed slopes, where Nardus mat grass and thyme mingled, giving way to thrift where the rain of sea spray was greatest. Black crowberry mingled with ling, its similar style foliage shinier, its succulent berries relished by ring ouzels, which we failed to see. There was little else apart from heath milkwort, tormentil and, quite incongruously, some tansy.

87. Black Crowberry and Heath Milkwort

As depth and waterlogging increased away from the cliff edges there was considerable slumping of peat hags - revealing slabs of shining white quartzite formerly hidden by the skin of heather. Exposed peat had the texture of black treacle pudding, just right for cutting out into neat slabs to keep the home fires burning.

A few sheep sought sustenance on the hills, all derivatives of longwool Scottish backfaces - the most hardy breed able to withstand the poor living and ferocious weather. Animals were furnished with single or double spiral horns.

Their close grazing of everything edible had left the way open for the wiry, flattened rosettes of heath rush (*Juncus squarrosus*) and shaggy Polytrichum moss. Unpalatable tufts of mat grass tweaked out in error were discarded, their bunched, wiry tufts crowned by needle leaves splaying out at right angles to the tough sheaths.

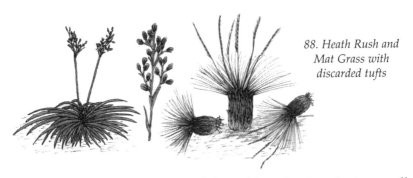

*88. Heath Rush and
Mat Grass with
discarded tufts*

Tiny ferns, English stonecrop and sheepsbit took refuge in stone walls, others among fleecy drifts of bog cotton or mats of the button leaves of marsh pennywort in the peat stained quagmires and gurgling runnels.

At the neatly lime-washed holiday complex of Keel we were not far from the deserted village of Sleavemore tucked into the base of the mountain of the same name. Its strung out row of abandoned cottages was reminiscent of the much photographed village of St. Kilda which the inhabitants abandoned in 1930.

Until that same time of 1930 Sleavemore saw an annual exodus of people and livestock to the mountain pastures in summer and back down again for the winter. This transhumance was the general practice in many parts of Wales in the old days and is still practised in Europe rather than waste the sweet grazings of alpine pastures which spend the winter under snow.

Sleavemore is credited with being the last place in the British Isles where this annual migration to make the most of seasonal assets was practised. Welsh husbandmen continue to summer their sheep and store cattle on the hills but dairy units and the making of butter and cheese stay in the valleys with the more mechanised farming community. The villagers of Sleavemore migrated permanently down the coast to Doogh.

Not surprisingly the greatest plant diversity was around the clustered houses and stone piers of the little settlements, but the hills called us away during our brief stay. It was glamorous scenery rather than floral diversity that captured the imagination of even the most ardent plant hunters on this rugged outlier of the European Union.

We walked to the foghorn accompaniment of a pair of ravens, the bubbling trill of distant curlews and the petulent mewing of gulls toying with the wind. Hurrying clouds rolled low over the glistening black peat hags, building up threateningly and then sidling away. It was time to adjourn to the delights of the gymkhana and noisy bustle in the grounds of Westport House on the adjacent mainland.

150

7

Manx - The Isle of Man
A LITTLE BIT OF EVERYTHING

Manx is a very different proposition from the islands visited so far, being a representative fragment of the British countryside, thirty two miles long by thirteen miles at its widest. Representative and yet unique. Its roots are Viking and it is self governing - its Tynwald the oldest parliament in the world, having met regularly for a thousand years.

It rises from the northern Irish Sea, almost equidistant from England, Scotland, Ireland and Wales, with Dublin only slightly further off than Belfast. Aligned with the Stranraer Peninsula in the north and the Isle of Anglesey in the south, with the English Lake District away to the east, it incorporates a little of each into its own special style. Shipping routes home in on Douglas, the capital, from Liverpool, North Lancashire and Ardrossan.

A wealth of public transport, embracing steam trains, electric trains and horse drawn trams, as well as buses and coaches, enables visitors to fly in rather than use the vehicle ferries, and not miss out on the tourist high spots. Thirty eight miles of road are set aside for a spell in June for the roaring, racing motor bikes competing in the annual TT (Tourist Trophy) races.

Population suffers none of the grinding poverty experienced on islands scattered along our Atlantic fringes. A rocky outlier in the south, about a mile in diameter, the Calf of Man, is more equivalent to those and is managed as a sea bird sanctuary by the Manx National Trust.

Our introductory visit in late May, 1998, coincided with the glory of flowering hawthorn frothing along the hedges throughout, and we were early enough to avoid the roar of the competing motor cycles so soon to begin.

We tried all the modes of transport, including shank's pony, but failed to discover the significance of the Manx trio of radiating legs. The most apt but unconfirmed explanation seemed to be that "Whatever way a Manxman falls, he always lands on his feet."

The island's geological foundation differs from Aran's limestone and Inishbofin's pre-cambrian. The Manx island backbone and most of the cliffs are of Ordovician slates. Snaefel and its fellow mountains are dotted

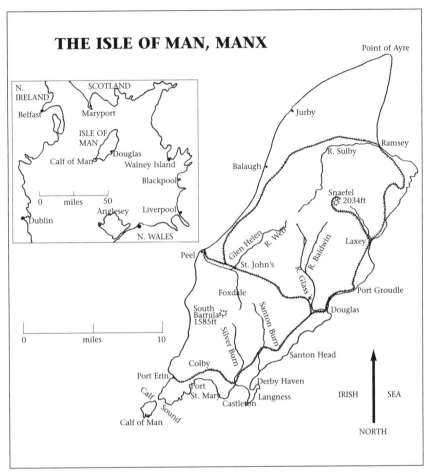

THE ISLE OF MAN, MANX

Point of Ayre

N. IRELAND
SCOTLAND
Belfast
Maryport
Jurby
ISLE OF MAN
Calf of Man
Douglas
Walney Island
Balaugh
R. Sulby
Ramsey
Blackpool
Snaefel
2034ft
0   miles   50
Anglesey
Liverpool
Dublin
N. WALES
Peel
Glen Helen
R. Wen
R. Baldwin
Laxey
St. John's
R. Glass
Foxdale
Port Groudle
0   miles   10
South Barrula
1585ft
Santon Burn
Douglas
Silver Burn
Santon Head
Colby
Port Erin
Port St. Mary
Derby Haven
Langness
Castletown
IRISH
SEA
Calf of Man
Calf Sound
NORTH

with boulders and outcrops of white quartz, appearing like resting sheep as we ascended the slopes, and the strata are threaded by white quartz veins. Carboniferous limestone dominates in the south and east around Castletown and granite and flints are to be found.

Wind strength is still a vital factor but not to the extent of eliminating trees altogether as on more oceanic outliers. Trees thrive in the bosky glens carved by the rivers, while those in more exposed sites can reach fair proportions during the summer, although suffering setbacks from salty gales during winter.

Wind trimmed trees appear to lean to leeward in submission, but the 'lean' is achieved by a drying out of buds to windward, leaving leeward ones to grow away and produce the lopsided shape. They did, indeed, bend in some of the sea winds we experienced, but not beyond the point of no return.

The island was at its most verdant during the latter part of May, the pastures an unbelievable green and some of them already mown for silage, the swaths stretching across the fields in neat rows to lose excess moisture before being compacted for winter forage. Most fields were bordered by a veritable candy floss of white blossoms as blackthorn gave way to whitethorn - the tree that is also named May for the month in which it can transform the landscape

Damp hollows harboured mauve drifts of milkmaid or lady's smock, recently afforded the rather overworked name of cuckoo flower - and just as the real cuckoos are disappearing from most of our landscapes. Buttercup swards into which they merged were at their most ebullient. The rural idyll transported us back to the mid twentieth century as a relief from the monotonous swards of perennial rye-grass which pervade so much of the kingdoms beyond these shores.

Rougher country was home to groves of yellow gorse shedding that pervasive perfume that reminded us of so many others all rolled into one. At summer's end a low blanket of bilberry or heather would take over some of the wilder parts. Lack of frost was apparent in the frequency of palms and New Zealand cabbage trees in private gardens and public parks. Well suited to withstand the salty winds were the Fuchsia and Escallonia in the hedgerows, as in so much of Western Ireland. Here, too, were dark flowered Hebe shrubs and wind tattered explosions of New Zealand flax with splaying orange flower spikes.

89. *New Zealand Cabbage Tree*

Little rivers carve steep valleys through the sea cliffs, these heavily wooded and appropriately referred to as glens. Bluebells and red campion, greater stitchwort and pignut imparted a cosy familiarity to those of us from kindlier climes. Yellow-green umbels of Alexanders burgeoned along the coastlands, with red valerian and wild garlic on the limestone.

Arable land was in good fettle, with thick stands of cereal seedlings pushing from fertile soil, sturdily sprouting potatoes, newly planted vegetables and brown sweeps of ploughland awaiting the drill. Pheasants were everywhere, also jackdaws, as in the Welsh Valleys, but

153

sometimes in company with hooded crows and red-legged daws or choughs.

Brashly succulent Hottentot fig *(Carpobrotus edule)* had taken hold and was advancing across coastal slopes near Douglas. Elsewhere were fine spreads of native spring squills and sheepsbit among thrift and sea campion.

In sampling the various wildlife habitats, we started on the extensive level country of the island's North. The softness of the surface sediment here shows on the map in the smoothness of the coastline in contrast to the jagged headlands and inlets of most of the rest.

The north-west coast centred around the sand dunes of Blue Point (which is not a point of any significance) stretches smoothly for twelve miles from just north of Peel in the south-west to Point of Ayre on the extreme northern tip, the smooth shore extending for another nine miles down the east side to beyond Ramsey. The four mile stretch of the "Ayres" proper is named for the old Norse for ridges of sand and gravel.

In fact there are significant sand cliffs at Jurby, these worn into neat alignment by the sea. Scattered rocks occur below high water mark and the sand cliffs give way northwards to dunes backing steep beaches. The shingle banks shelve sharply seawards beyond the lighthouse on the point proper, shifting in currents sweeping round the point and rendering bathing dangerous.

They are of glacial gravels, much in demand as aggregates for building, and some of the depressions from which quantities have been removed are a little reminiscent of Dungeness. Less disturbed parts form undulating ridges of heather moor, studded with gorse bushes. The approach road passed between a shallow hollow with regenerating vegetation and a landfill site where a high mesh fence prevented most of the domestic waste from escaping, spurred on by playful winds. Scavenging gulls were in full voice as they took first pickings from the dump. Apparently prisoners were employed to gather up debris which made it over the fence.

The tall lighthouse tower, banded in red and white, was automated, like all the rest nowadays, and the associated buildings converted to private housing. We lingered, watching for ferry boats plying from Douglas to Belfast or Ardrossan in Scotland. That northern land was said to be nineteen and a half miles away, the Cumbrian mountains further, but clearly visible across the ultramarine expanse.

The low heath to landward was heavily rabbited, constant nibbling of young heather shoots causing much to revert to fine grasses with English stonecrop and heath lichens taking over where even those were worn threadbare. A particularly extensive warren was situated on a spreading mound and several of the grassed anthills were thickly strewn with twice defecated rabbit pellets, where the gregarious creatures met to socialise and exchange pheromones.

Pied wagtails appreciated the short grass areas, as they do golfing greens, for the easy pecking. Ringed plovers puttered around on the pebbles and common terns were dipping for fish offshore. Rooks and magpies tended towards the bordering cereal and potato crops, sparrows, starlings and wood pigeons were more interested in the landfill site but had to concede priority to the squabbling gulls.

90. Wood Pigeons

Ramsay, towards the change from smooth sands to scenic rockscapes on the north-east coast, was a haven for pleasure craft and yachts of all sorts. It lies at the mouth of the Sulby River and has a half mile long pier from which line fishermen can practise their craft. These and their boat-borne contemporaries had the chance of catching the usual inshore flatfish, dogfish, mackerel, pollack and the not so welcome occasional conger eel.

Boating can be enjoyed on a smaller scale on the lake in the forty acre Mooragh Park. All the usual seaside pursuits can be pursued in this pleasant watering hole where shelter from the prevalent south westerlies ensures a proliferation of colourful bedding plants, including some of the not so hardy, as well as safe, sandy bathing.

Maughold Head is the most easterly point on the Isle of Man, protruding sufficiently to have been accorded another lighthouse. It is three hundred and eighty five feet high and commands fine views up and down the coast. Laxey, seven miles further south, was a centre of the woollen industry in the past and is famous for its mighty water wheel, the largest in Britain with a diameter of seventy two and a half feet and a circumference of two hundred and seventeen feet. It was constructed in 1854 in the narrow river valley a mile or so from the sea, to pump water out of the lead mines which burrowed under Snaefell Mountain. Silver was associated with the lead - as in the ancient mines lost in the beechwoods near my home on the outskirts of Cardiff.

Laxey Wheel was still functional and we watched in admiration as it completed each revolution in thirty seconds, flashing its new red paint beside the iron stairway spiralling up the white tower alongside to an overhead gangway leading across the top of its orbit. An alternative name for this popular industrial showpiece is The Lady Isabella, after the wife of the island governor in residence at the time of building.

The river falls away steeply into the little harbour which dries out at low tide and the immediate environs of the wheel are green with rank herbage and shrubs, later to be engulfed by bracken, with colourful gorse bushes stretching away up the grassy slopes. We explored the mine tunnels open to the public and followed some of the mine trails.

Peering into the crumbling ruins of the old engine house we spotted two occupied birds' nests. Pied wagtails were tucked into a vertical crevice eight inches high and great tits had taken over a horizontal crack two inches wide. A pair of chaffinches lingered nearby, one carrying nesting material. but not letting on where it was taking its burden.

It was good to see pied flycatchers in these ferny woods, so reminiscent of those of Central Wales. Goldcrests were as confiding as always and a pair of grey wagtails foraged along the tinkling stream. It was hoodies, not carrion crows that flapped importantly across the ground-bustling blackbirds and robin.

Stone walls hereabouts were more substantial than the loosely piled, wind-letting ones of Ireland and supported a fine wall flora. Most attractive were the turrets of white bells sprouting from among the fleshy disc leaves of wall pennywort and dwarfing the pink-tinged flowers of the related English stonecrop alongside. With them were three spleenwort ferns: shiny fronds of the black, elegant ones of the maidenhair and neat wedge-shaped segments of the little wall rue. Some of the polypody ferns had escaped from the walls, their scaly rhizomes winding up neighbouring tree trunks to perch far above our heads on mossy boughs.

91. Great Tits

Noble dame's violet and red valerian lightened our path as we walked back to the church and railway station. A farmyard bantam had brought her brood of day old chicks out onto the highway, relieved, no doubt, that her long broody period was at an end. The gathering of them up and shooing her back to safety occupied us as we awaited our next transport.

This had been the electric railway, but we changed here onto the steam powered mountain railway winding up from Laxey Glen to Snaefel. At 2,036 feet, this is the island's highest mountain, overtopping the next highest, the South Barrula Mountain, by 449 feet. Dipping only to cross the route to be taken by the TT contestants the following week, we were mostly in open moorland country, more in keeping with that of the Western Isles.

And so was the climate! The bitter wind blasting across the summit came as a shock after the balmy sunshine experienced in Laxey's kindly glen. Vegetation up here was kept short by black-faced mountain longwools and how glad they must have been of that dense, water repellent fleece.

This was a closely grazed bilberry moor, with splaying deer sedge and needle-leaved grasses but very little heather. The low growth was topped in parts by drifts of soft rush, affording a modicum of shelter for nesting meadow pipits. Boggy patches spawned small flies for the swallows but these had to swoop low to intercept them where the wind was marginally less boisterous.

92. *Bilberry or Whortleberry*

The view embraced the old mine and a reservoir, but we became engulfed in thin cloud, which rendered the distant view hazy. No road leads right to the summit, but there was a cafe for rail passengers and walkers, where we were pleased enough to take shelter after battling through to the trig point at the top.

Groudle Glen, a few miles down the coast, seemed to belong to a different world - a May time Manx fairyland where shade was an asset rather than otherwise. Treading softly on fallen leaves, we zig-zagged down to where the little river sparkled over clean pebbles and water-smoothed rock. Seepage from clifflets green with liverworts nurtured banks of ferns and bluebells, peppered with the white of wood sorrel and stitchwort among spent wood Anemone leaves

Another red painted water wheel, little brother to the Laxey Wheel, was fixed in the current alongside a tall, narrow timbered workroom cum

93. Pink Purslane

cottage with a brief balcony in front, the building tucked into the sloping shingly shore.

Where the gorge opened out below the water wheel, the banks were draped with pink purslane *(Montia sibirica or Claytonia alsinoides)* - a beauty of the North and West which we do not see in South Wales, where its only close relative is the humble water blinks. The flowers clustered round ancient, fern crowned tree boles reflecting the dappled light filtering through lime, ash and oak. Their colour matched that of the ragged robin and red campion.

The river was alive with brook trout, up to a handspan long, each deeper pool harbouring a shoal headed upstream to maintain position while intercepting any goodies coming down, or flipping out in a flurry of silver as they reached for laggard mayflies fallen from the dancing, sunlit swarms above. A grey wagtail pottered over the pebble banks and a blue-tailed damselfly sunbathed on an Angelica leaf.

In a quieter pool, where yellow Irises stood tall among spearing leaves, were royal ferns, upstanding clumps, the young golden fronds excelling each other in their reach for the light. Royal indeed, this is a rarity in South Wales nowadays after being filched in the past for gardens.

Where river worn pebbles merged with those rounded by the sea, the trout headed more determinedly upstream, lest they be pickled before even aspiring sea trout were ready for the change. Pink Rhododendron blossoms gave way to the red of salt tolerant Fuchsia and the white umbels of rowan to those of may.

Two choughs commuted between feeding sites, calling their name, to settle among thrift and sea campion and probe the salted turf for grubs. A pair of rock pipits divided their attention between the driftline and the silverweed/mayweed/cleavers carpet of the beach crest, while hooded crows went about their business overhead. Offshore a pair of mallard flew in to join the mallard drake which had seduced a white farmyard duck, with her apparent whole hearted approval.

It was as warm on the lichen covered Ordovician slate as in the sheltered glen - a blissful change from the biting north winds that swept across the island that week. It missed this corner, where a yellowhammer among the gorse complained of a lack of cheese - also the low headland where we lunched among bird's-foot trefoil, spring squill and sheepsbit, helped by a lone, silent gull, which had shadowed our every movement since we emerged from the glen.

Orange tips and whites of the wood yielded to peacocks and common blues. One of many small heaths returned repeatedly to bask on a small stone at our feet, the male and female wall butterflies preferring larger ones nearby. Only twenty six of Britain's sixty eight butterfly species have been recorded on the Isle of Man.

Hard clay on the cliff path was riddled with the nesting burrows of solitary bees, each a few inches from the next. The busybody builders buzzed to and fro, their pollen baskets laden, to build up the marzipan balls of bee bread that would nourish their progeny. Passing human feet made no impression on the unyielding matrix of the path. How would the young bees fare digging their way out on emergence from the pupae?

Groudle Glen offered two contrasting habitats, each vibrant with colour and scuttling with life - beetles, bugs, bumble bees, flies, in and out of the water, a dripping, ferny paradise and a sun drenched natural rock garden juxtaposed, with no hint of pollution from the amateur-run mini steam railway curving round above. This we followed for a while.

The railway had opened in 1896 to serve a zoo at Sea Lion Rocks. After closure during the war it continued to run until 1962 when it was scrapped and the track dismantled. Twenty years later volunteers came together to restore and reopen it, section by section, from 1986 on. Its motive power was the original loco, the Sea Lion, a green engine pulling two dark red carriages. The line follows the coast from Sea Lion Rocks to the mouth of the river and then heads up along the wooded flank of the valley south of the stream.

Douglas, but a short hop down the coast from here, is the island's capital, where the Manx Electric Railway from the north meets the Manx Steam Railway from the south. Formerly another line crossed from here to Peel in the west and looped northward to connect with the electric line at Ramsay, but that had been closed before our visit. Only the Groudle Glen Railway is operated and owned by volunteers.

A ticket purchased for eighty pence entitled us to all day travel on the horse drawn trams had we wished to shuttle repeatedly back and forth along the promenade. This service started in 1876 and is said to employ seventy horses, which are pensioned off into a grassy retreat at the end of their working lives. The steadily trotting Clydesdales, having run the route so many times, moved neatly between the tramlines with little or no guidance from their 'drivers'. Only at the Onchon Head destination did they edge sideways for a well earned slurp from the proffered bucket of water.

The town stretches for two miles around the curve of Douglas Bay, and we were domiciled near the southern end at the Berkeley House Hotel on Loch Promenade. A little way offshore St. Mary's Island reared from the water bearing a castellated folly - a central flag-flying stone tower flanked by two lesser ones. A smaller rock nearby was a danger to shipping when it disappeared at high tide and was marked by a tepee buoy.

Away to its right was the main harbour under Douglas Head at the mouth of the Baldwin and Glass Rivers, with its traffic of ferries, freighters and fishing boats. The long breakwater, topped by boulders, stretched nor-nor-east, parallel to the shore, with a shorter quay to landward. This was visible from our balcony, which was a fine place to sit sketching and watching the world go by.

A long dry spell and unusual late frosts had hindered the planting of flower beds along the front, but plots of Gazzanias, Petunias and busy Lizzies were gradually materialising.

Restless herring gulls shouted their displeasure from town roofs by day and could be spotted in the early morning tweaking newly planted African marigolds from window boxes in search of grubs. If these were vine weevils they were welcome but plants had to be re-installed after their visits. Jackdaws were busy on the beach, mostly hauling sand hoppers or fly larvae from the piled seaweed. Rooks, starlings, sparrows and pigeons were also finding goodies down there to keep them occupied.

The tide withdrew a long way, exposing acres of sand, softening in its lower reaches where it was liberally tunnelled by lugworms - a favourite bait of longshore fishermen. Paired dimpled pits and coiled worm casts marked the intake and exit of each U shaped burrow. Rock which protruded under Onchan Head must have been close below the surface over much of the rest, because the clumps of brown wrack scattered across the sand were firmly anchored to something more substantial underneath.

Stalking silently among wallflowers and bellflowers in the town gardens behind the theatre was a tail-less tabby cat. Of course, the famous Manx, occasionally locally called a rumpy. A specimen showing this mutation way back in time had been taken into custody and used to sire a line of progeny which bred true. With no tails to wave in anger, they must express their emotions at the front end.

The progeny have been given official protection, the continuance of the breed ensured by a cattery in Nobles Park, Douglas. They come in all coat colours, not just tabby. Has the loss of one of their appendages been compensated for by the island logo's extra leg?

The other domestic animal that is specific to the Isle of Man is the Loghtan sheep, a few of which we saw in our travels. This ancient Manx breed is unmistakable with its two, four or even six horns and medium brown fleece. Unthrifty by modern sheep farming standards, it was in danger of extinction by the 1960s, but the residue was saved by the Manx National Trust.

94 Loghtan Sheep

Five animals were removed to run on the Calf of Man in 1969 and they proved their suitability to local conditions by increasing to twenty eight by 1973.

Native mammals are scarce, many not getting far enough beyond the land bridge from Europe after the Ice Age to arrive here before the further land bridge to Manx was engulfed by rising sea level. There are thus no badgers, foxes, squirrels, moles, voles, snakes or toads.

The fecund rabbits made up for the paucity of other nibblers and there are a few long-tailed field mice and pygmy shrews. Sadly for the ground-nesting sea-birds on the Calf of Man, brown rats came ashore there, probably from a sinking ship, in the early nineteenth century. Pipistrelle, long-eared and Daubenton's bats have been caught in mist nets by bird ringers on the Calf.

The National Trust Amamon Museum was a boon on our wet day, its presentation of genuine history flavoured with a soupçon of myth and legend. A less permanent but impressive building was being erected on our last day for a Hondas motor bike presentation, some of the bikes already zooming up on us.

A number thirty bus took us to the steam train station for our jaunts south - to Port St. Mary on the first occasion. The engine blundered rowdily through the tranquil spring countryside, belching the clouds of black smoke that send tingles of pleasure down the spines of railway buffs but are generally not tolerated in this age of air fresheners and smoking bans except as a tourist gimmick. There are still those who enjoy the nostalgia of leaning from carriage windows to withdraw sprinkled with black smuts.

95. Hooded Crows

Despite all the years of transit of these mechanical monsters, the rabbits and pheasants had not become inured to the din and scuttled for cover at our passing. A heron winged away to quieter waters. Only the hovering kestrel and busy corvids ignored us.

Homely backyard scenes speeding past reminded us of a bygone age. A little gathering of goats, sharing a trough of fodder with a donkey, were ignoring a magpie sneaking titbits from under their noses. This was evidently a 'free for all' with no serious competition from so inferior an interloper. The bird of the day must have been the albino house sparrow, standing out blatantly among its decently camouflaged fellows.

We alighted at Port St. Mary Station and, as the train drew away, the busy little possie of goldfinches returned to the station platform and were there to greet us on our return. Dropping nearly to sea level, we followed the walk around the headland separating East Bay from the main town and docks. Jetties stretched seawards, the two longest with warning lights at their tips, sheltering a busy holiday harbour.

This is the island's main sailing centre, with deep water close inshore for yachts and fishing boats. It was built on a rocky section of shore, but a sandy beach stretched eastwards around the long sweep of Carricky Bay. Tidal pools were exposed at low water and the strand was backed by a pleasant grassy promenade with ornamental shrubs and spots for sitting in the sun when the wind was not at gale force as it was at the time. Past the docks and fishermen's quarters, we followed the promenade to crouch behind a stone shelter out of the wind to eat our sandwiches.

Neat round holes bored in the boulders topping the long stone wall intrigued us. They must have been made by rosy-nosed rock borers, Hiatella. On this corner of the island limestone forms horizontal shelves providing easier boring for these industrious invertebrates. Although sufficiently solluble to be dissolved away by certain animal enzymes, its seems that these boring bivalves penetrate by mechanical rather than chemical means. There were a few outcrops of the predominant Ordovician slates, with bold quartz veins but no animal burrows.

A white goose was preeening on the shore, ignoring the jackdaws pecking among the driftweed in search of non borers. Rock sea spurrey, scurvy grass and tiny sea fern grass on seaside walls gave way to spleen-worts, polypody and red valerian as we moved inland to return by the upper road.

Along the lower road were cottages with little walled gardens, some very attractive and on steep slopes not visible from the cottage windows below, where lived those who had tended them, but they were a visual feast for those leaning over the wall above. We lingered awhile in the Seamen's Memorial Gardens, sharing a bench with boxes of young plants about to be set out by volunteers.

Our return train journey afforded fine views of the blocky, castellated eminence of Castle Rushen. This medieval fort is in the centre of Castletown, which was the island's capital until 1874 and where the lower house of the Tynwald met. Rushen Abbey is at Ballasalla, the next station along the line. This town has no harbour, unlike most on the island, which are set around the coast, having been built when Manx depended largely on its sea-born trade.

Another train on another day took us a little further along the same line to Port Erin. Tortuous streets led down to sea level where, once again, was a row of fishermen's cottages, leaving the high road to the tourist hotels. St. Catherine's Well, a small freshwater spring seeping from the cliff face, sustained the dwellers by the sea before more sophisticated water systems were laid on above.

We were back on the Ordovician slates here, featured as towering cliffs to seaward of the seven hundred and sixty six feet high Bradda Hill, which bore Milner's Tower, a useful sea mark for shipping. The nineteenth century resort was built at the northern end of a sandy bay and offers all the pleasures expected on a seaside holiday.

For me, having been a student of Professor Lily Newton, Britain's seaweed queen and author of the state of the art tome for the identification of marine algae at the time, Port Erin was pre-eminently the site of the famous marine biological station which we had heard so much about in lectures. Part was open to the public and we had hoped, as ex protegees, that we might see a little more, but it was not to be. This was the May bank holiday and all doors were firmly barred. The nearest we got was to watch enviously as groups of students in wet suits loaded compressed air cylinders into small inflatables powered by outboard motors and headed out from the jetty steps for a dive.

We mooched to the end of the concrete standing where countless flippered feet had nurtured a classic 'lawn' of buck's horn plantain with

96. Vernal Squill and Golden Saxifrage

sea plantain, thrift and dwarf Danish scurvy grass. Primroses burgeoned on the grassy slope behind, with vernal squill and sea campion. Golden saxifrage carpeted a mossy seepage supporting Angelica and grading out through tufted and bush vetch.

The concrete was littered with scraps of crab carapaces and shells among oval gull pellets consisting of fish bones. A herring gull left the group playing in the eddies above the flowery bank to alight and cough up another. Choughs were resting on the headland and a fulmar petrel shot past, undeviating as the flight of an arrow.

Returning to town with its little gardens, we explored the sands. Whelk egg cases like fossilized frogspawn had washed in from the sub-littoral, to be caught up in tangles of bootlace weed. This last (*Chorda filum*) I have recently seen referred to by the more evocative name of mermaid's tresses. Here, as at Douglas, a broad intertidal zone was exposed on the ebb. We watched the tide withdrawing beyond the headland and followed it down to investigate the exposed oarweed beds.

Because of the closure of the western loop of the railway, our visit to Peel and its mighty castle on the west coast was by public bus service. Peel developed as the island's main fishing port. Each July Viking longships ride at anchor in the bay, as a colourful reminder of the initial invasion by Norsemen in AD 798.

Fishing is less important now than previously, but herring boats still pull into the harbour behind the breakwater at the mouth of the River Neb. The herrings are kippered for export and we were able to witness the various stages of processing. Odours are said to be more evocative of the past than sounds or sights. Few are more powerful than that of kippering, and my thoughts were whisked back to a childhood visit to the kipper curers of Mallaig at the end of the long scenic road from Fort William in the Western Highlands.

One of today's main commercial fisheries is the dredging of scallops from sandy inshore waters, these, too, for export. The British are not great shellfish eaters and scallops do not rank high among the few molluscs that we imbibe in any quantity. Recreational fishing from small boats and from the breakwater extending beyond the castle walls, embraces mackerel, pollack, conger eel, skate and other flatfish, also mullet, which tolerate the ingress of fresh water from the Neb.

A road leads across the causeway to St. Patrick's Isle, sheltering the waters behind from the caprices of the Irish Sea. The afterthought of land at its end is encircled by the curtain wall of Peel Castle, with its evenly spaced turrets. The castle dates back to before the first Viking invasion, when it was captured by the intruding Norsemen. To help prevent a repeat, the perimeter wall was built in the fourteenth century.

Most of the ground within was occupied by the neatly manicured lawns which characterise renovated ruins tidied up to delight visitors - particularly those from the newly settled lands Down Under and in the Far West. Ruins of the thirteenth century St. Germains Cathedral huddle towards the landward shore and a massive round tower rises above the fretted skyline created by the great wall.

Tortuous winding streets of the town savoured somewhat of a Cornish fishing village. The promenade curved gently round an arc of white sand lapped by the jostling waves of a fretful ocean. Oyster catchers piped distractedly from the tide's edge and gulls challenged the malignant wind that blew their feathers out of alignment.

We escaped the breeze-blown coast on our second visit, opting to explore the river, which flows northward on its last lap before losing itself in the salty expanse. Crossing over at the head of the harbour, we walked up the western, castle, side, but the sheltering trees soon gave way to open fields. Grass and underbrush streamed to leeward and hooded crows came rollicking downwind at high speed, seemingly out of control, but probably relishing the free ride as much as the gulls, which practise daily on cliff updraughts. Most of the small birds were grounded.

We chickened out and crossed back to follow the east bank along the old railway line. This was now geared to walkers, with display boards, newly planted trees and the occasional seat. Mallard and moorhen pursued their watery business in the welcome protection of drooping bank vegetation.

A few butterflies had ventured out in the brief oases of calm. Here were orange tips and whites, common blues and wall browns, along with gently buzzing bees in various shapes and sizes. Such havens were rare. We thought nostalgically of the magic of Groudle Glen and dived into a bistro to warm up before catching the bus back.

We had kept our eyes open for the special Isle of Man cabbage (*Coincya monensis*), which resembles charlock more closely than traditional cabbages. It occurs spasmodically here and along the nearby Cumbrian coast and further afield, but we failed to find it. The subspecies, *wrightii*, is even more restricted in its range, occurring only on the island of Lundy off the North Devon coast. The Manx plant, like the Manx shearwater, is named after the island but is commoner elsewhere. Many have sought the Manx shearwater in the bird sanctuary of the Calf of Man, but have failed to locate any nests.

97. *Isle of Man Cabbage*

This, the Calf of Man, was to be the highlight of our visit - a true seabird island where wildlife took priority over the affairs of humankind. Once again, it was not to be! Boats plied across the intervening strait carrying members of the public to the Calf even in the birds' nesting season when the weather was right, but the weather was not right on any day during our stay.

This south west corner was almost our first port of call, leaving plenty more days for a repeat visit, but the spiteful wind did not abate all week. I had to content myself with an illustrated talk about the island by the ornithologist warden several years later in far off Cheltenham at a reunion of the "Friends of Skokholm and Skomer Islands",

From the carpark on the mainland we had views of two groups of Atlantic seals, thirty three in all, lolling on the rocks of Little Sound - a tantalising taste of what might have been, had we made it to Manx's wildlife gem. This, apparently, is an average sighting, although as many as seventy are sometimes seen together, occasionally with an odd, snub-nosed common seal among the Dalmation faced greys.

Beyond Little Sound was the double island of Kitterland, this separated from the Calf proper by "The Sound", in which lies the lesser islet of Thousla. Shags commuted across the ruffled water between and pearly grey kittiwakes, their legs dangling for better aerial control in the capricious wind. Straight winged, cruciform fulmars planed down the air corridors and great black-backed gulls stood atop coastal lookouts, lording it over all the rest.

The turf of our headland, worn short by countless human feet and showered with sea spray on occasion, resembled a bird island turf

98. Fulmars

manicured by rabbits. Spring squill, thrift and sea campion mingled with bright patches of bird's-foot trefoil and pignut with English stonecrop and violets.

The Calf, hanging off the south-west corner of the main island, occupies 250 hectares. It is almost entirely bounded by slate cliffs rising to over three hundred feet, with no sandy holiday beaches and few pebble strands. Eleven species of sea birds nest on the cliffs, with guillemots on offlying stacks. Manx shearwaters are now sparse here.

This, our only resident shearwater, was first described here in 1678 and history has it that some lived here as far back as 1014. Thriving during the Middle Ages, the colony was subsequently decimated by the taking of the young birds for food and there were few or none left by the start of the nineteenth century. Odd birds have been seen visiting, but few, if any, nest in modern times.

Auks, too, reach but a fraction of their former numbers, but the largest of them all may have lived here back in the mists of time. A little over thirty years ago great auk bones were excavated in a cave at Perwick about three miles away. The extinction of Europe's greatest sea birds, at the hands of hungry sailors, is almost as well documented as the death of the dodo in far off Mauritius.

The Calf was leased to the Manx National Trust in 1951 and has been wardened as a nature reserve since farming ceased in 1958, The bird observatory opened the following year and has excelled as a ringing station for passing migrants, with awesome numbers of birds handled in subsequent years, leading to recoveries from places as widely dispersed as South-west Africa and Greenland. At least fifty five species of birds nest on the island, with large contingents of common land birds passing through on spring and autumn passage.

Of the sea and shore birds herring gulls are much the most numerous, numbering around two thousand pairs in the 1970s. Kittiwakes were next among the gulls, decreasing from seven hundred and twenty pairs to a hundred and seventy five, concurrently with the building up of a new colony a mile or so away on the main island's east coast. Some three hundred pairs of shags nest. 1973 figures for auks were a hundred and twenty five pairs of razorbills, a hundred of guillemots but only thirty pairs of puffins, with sixty pairs of fulmar petrels and nineteen of oyster catchers, these varying from year to year. Far and away the most numerous passerines are meadow pipits and wrens, with rock pipits, starlings, linnets and blackbirds next in abundance.

Livestock farming had been carried out in the shelter of the island's central valley cut by a stream dammed at its southern end as a water supply. Most of the rest to either side is heather moor, with a few fields created on the western flank near the upper and lower lighthouses and the Stack.

As on the Pembrokeshire Islands, the heather is being invaded by bracken - sheets of bluebells preceeding the unfurling of the fronds in June and generous pockets of April primroses heralding this azure tide in May.

Rabbits took over from the farm livestock in keeping the fields neatly trimmed until the population was devastated by Myxomatosis in the sixties and seventies. Their population ebbs and flows with outbreaks of the disease, allowing taller plants to invade when their numbers are low.

Clifftop plants again conform with those of the Welsh Islands in their dazzling pink spreads of thrift and tiny subordinates such as thyme, centaury and eyebright. All survive the rabbits by remaining small and huddling in the shelter of less palatable 'toughies'.

Butterflies and moths have been studied, the latter caught in profusion in the vicinity of the still functional lighthouse, which attracts moths as surely as it attracts birds - like an outsize mercury vapour moth trap. In fact the modern lighthouse, at three hundred and five feet or ninety four metres above sea level and operational since 1968, has proved to inflict little damage on migrating birds. It is, indeed, thought to have a 'pulling power' attracting night migrants which might otherwise pass by without alighting.

8
Walney Island, Cumbria
DUNE, STORM BEACH, SALTMARSH & WETLAND

Walney Island lies near the boundary between Lancashire and the Lake District and is on the same latitude as the Calf of Man, but some sixty miles to its east. Like the Calf it is subjected to the sweeping tides of the Irish Sea, boosted by the Atlantic skirting Northern Ireland, but it yields to this force much more readily.

It is a different type of island altogether and much more vulnerable to marine erosion. Essentially a long sandbar, often topped by dunes, it is bordered by uninterrupted sandy beaches, some backed by pebble storm beaches or fronted by muddy saltmarshes. Like Achill Island, it is connected to the mainland by a road bridge spanning the separating strait.

The point of contact is Barrow-in-Furness, which developed around Furness Abbey, founded by Cistercian monks in 1127, its blocky ruins still to be seen. The monks were the first to smelt the local iron ore and build the fleet of trading ships which helped to make their foundation second only in wealth and importance to Fountains Abbey in Yorkshire.

More modern furnaces were smelting ore in the eighteenth century and shipping iron to furnaces throughout the country. With Walney Island forming a first class natural breakwater across the harbour entrance, Barrow developed as a modern ship building port. Royal Navy ships were fashioned here, from the old ironclads to HMS "Invincible" and from Britain's earliest submarine to today's nuclear powered craft.

The Isle of Walney is linear, a straight beach of ten miles bounding its western side, with mile long sand spits dipping in towards the mainland at both ends. Less than four hundred yards wide in places, excessive storms have sent waves pounding right across it on occasion.

Sea level rise with global warming could prove crucial here. Even without extra warmth, the predicted storms could wreak havoc on a coast as fragile as this. Recent studies have shown that more than a hundred hectares (250 acres) of low lying coastal fringe land are being lost to the sea every year in the UK. Though more crucial in the South-east, Walney is situated on the fulcrum of the gentle rise or sinking of the

169

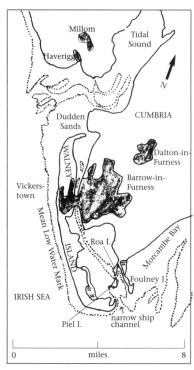

WALNEY ISLAND

A 12 mile long sandspit, bird observatory and nature reserve. Connected to Cumbria at Barrow-in-Furness

Millom
Tidal Sound
Haverigg
Dudden Sands
CUMBRIA
WALNEY
Dalton-in-Furness
Barrow-in-Furness
Vickers-town
Mean Low Water Mark
ISLAND
Roa I.
Morcambe Bay
Foulney I
IRISH SEA
narrow ship channel
Piel I.

0   miles   8

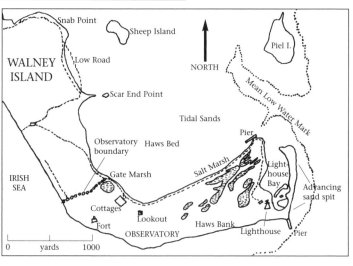

WALNEY ISLAND

Snab Point
Sheep Island
Low Road
NORTH
Piel I.
Scar End Point
Mean Low Water Mark
Tidal Sands
Observatory boundary
Haws Bed
Pier
Gate Marsh
Salt Marsh
Light-house Bay
IRISH SEA
Advancing sand spit
Cottages
Lookout
Fort
OBSERVATORY
Haws Bank
Lighthouse
Pier

0   yards   1000

170

land as it recovers from its former burden of ice. Surges fed from the Atlantic could shift thousands of tons of sand overnight.

The sandbar is broadest at the end of the connecting bridge where the garden city style dormitory suburb of Vickerstown was built at the beginning of the twentieth century to house the iron workers and ship builders. This dynamic coastline has none of Ireland's massive cliffs to thwart the onslaught of the sea. Its pebbles, clay and sand, brought by ice flow and wind blow, have few defences and move stone by stone or grain by grain at the whim of the moon motivated tides.

Along this stretch of Britain's coast the twice daily ebb and flow reveal the most extensive tidal sands in the entire countrry. The sandspits advancing inexorably landwards at each end of Walney Island are as illustrative of this dynamism as the probably better known growing sandbars running parallel to the equally mobile coast of East Anglia.

Two fifths of the island in the north was occupied by open country, connected to the mainland at low tide by a pebble tipped tongue of the vast sand flats leading into the estuary of the River Duddon. The three fifths south of the bridge and township was almost uninhabited and separated at all states of the tide from the mainland. A quite narrow channel, bordered on both sides by sand flats at ebb tide, is sufficiently deep to form the main shipping channel into Barrow Docks. At full tide the open water entry is two miles wide.

The inward turned sand spit at the island's south-east extremity is growing in length at a rate of up to seventeen feet a year, creating progressively more shelter to Haws Bed which occupies the bay in its lee. The coast stretches north from here to form the western shore of Morecambe Bay.

The southern part of the island is designated as a bird reserve and is home to one of the largest nesting colonies of herring gulls and lesser black-backs in Europe. It comes under the jurisdiction of the Lancashire and Lake District's Naturalists' Trusts and interest has been added in recent decades by immigrant eider ducks.

Approach is along a paved road from Vickerstown or North Seale as far as the municipal rubbish tip. Then comes a rougher section to about three kilometres north of the Bird Observatory, which is based in three old cottages formerly occupied by coastguards and their families. A fork in the track offers two routes on the ebb, but the lower branch goes under water at most tides, when the upper farm road needs to be used.

Lying south-west of the Lake District, the two kilometre long nature reserve forms the most westerly point of Morecambe Bay, famous for its cockles and infamous for the tragic loss of life of twenty one migrant Chinese cockle pickers on the incoming tide of 5th February 2004.

No less than a hundred and seventeen square miles of wet sand are exposed in Morecambe Bay on an average ebb tide. To cross on foot would entail a walk of ten miles and is not to be attemprted by the uninitiated as the advancing flood surges across the levels faster than a person could keep ahead of it.

Three rivers snaking across the sands carve themselves new deep channels at will, possibly crossing to the opposite flank in as little as forty eight hours and confusing the system of laurel branches that the official guide uses to mark the safe foot passages, although his canny knowledge of water movements and ripples around sand banks enable him to guide parties of walkers safely across.

99. Godwits

Along with the cockles moving over rocks under the fickle sands are other bivalves, shrimps, crabs and marine worms - a veritable feast for wading birds and sea duck. Notable takers are oyster catchers, curlew, godwit, knot and dunlin.

I was there with a party of Cardiff Naturalists in 1965. As a change from craggy mountains and deep, cold lakes we had botanised among the lime-loving plants of Humphrey Head, a limestone promontary rising a hundred and seventy three feet above the far flung Morecambe Bay sands. The more stable sands of Walney called.

The parent rock at Walney is New Red Sandstone lying unconformably on much older rock, but this is apparent only as 'scars' or rocky mounds overtopping the drifting sand of the outer beach and as dark red pebbles in the mix of different hues on the storm beaches. Stacks and islets peeped from sand or water on the inland side, but the bones of the land were mostly coated by glacial drift. First came the boulder clay, producing a thin covering of soil, and then a layer of blown sand. Of limited agricultural value, the latter supports poor pasture for grazing animals rather than crops. Free range cattle, red, black, piebald and skewbald, more often referred to as red and white or roan, roamed the dunes and sandy grassland among the nesting gulls and there were a few ewes with lambs at foot.

Although the gull nesting season was well advanced on this, the first of June, the farm animals were still suffering frequent dive bombing attacks from both gull species, although they seemed little perturbed by the constant harrying. Perhaps they had become inured to fiercer defensive sorties by birds during the onset of nesting, when the intruders might have been sufficiently intimidated to retreat to where there was less liklihood of trampling on nests.

During the latter part of the twentieth century sand and gravel were being removed on an industrial scale as aggregates for building projects. Huge conical mounds of sand and pebbles spewed from the hoppers formed favoured gathering grounds and lookout points for off duty adult gulls and newly fledged young - seemingly more of the latter at this season, merging into the gravelly patches with their tweedy brown plumage.

More significant for the well being of the nature reserve were cavities left by the giant diggers. These collected rain and seepage to form a useful mix of freshwater ponds and marshes and deeper bodies of brackish water attracting a diversity of wildfowl in winter. A wet area surrounded by ten metre high dunes had become richly vegetated and was a favourite stopping off retreat for pasing migrants and residents in need of cover. The ever growing landward-reaching sandspit protects a tidal lagoon sheltered from all winds except those from the north.

Sand dunes, still shaggy with the marram grass which had slowed the progress of the blowing sand in the first instance, provided the main nesting area for the gulls. The central marsh catered for waders and the amalgam of pools for wildfowl, these moving out onto the tidal flats to probe for molluscs and crustaceans as the water drains away. Heligoland traps to capture passerines for ringing were in use in the better vegetated areas.

Piel Island is the largest outcrop in the water to landward of the nature reserve. It can be approached from Haws bank by a somewhat circuitous route over the sands at low water of springs, with shipping passing to its north, and is included in the reserve. Being ideally placed to defend the entry into Barrow Harbour, a castle was built there in the twelfth century to do just that.

Passing ships showed the deep water channel to be very close to the ruins that we were seeing beyond the sand sifting gear on the reserve. This was not, however, the first edifice, but a fortress and warehouse for trade goods from the abbey, built a hundred years later by the monks.

Here they stored wool from their extensive flocks, wine and various items of food. In 1486 Piel Island was the landing point of Irish and Flemish invaders. Maybe if Walney's southern sand spit keeps on growing, it may join up with it.

At present the usual approach is by boat from Roa Island on the other side of the shipping channel. Roa is an island no longer, but the tip of a narrow spit from the mainland. The larger Foulney Island, again, is no longer an island but a two mile long arm of land leading from the other. It is famed among bird watchers for its nesting terns - a flock which it shares with Walney Island - in accordance with the somewhat fickle nesting activities of these spritely birds.

Arthur Evans, the warden, met us at the old Coastguard Station and conducted us around the man-made features of the reserve and the industrial plant. The nearby lighthouse, set as high as the limited dunes allowed, had an angular, probably hexagonal tower alongside the slate - roofed living quarters.

The gulls were all around us in a caterwauling mob, shrieking blue murder as they dived to attack, with intent to intimidate rather than wound and scoring near misses rather than actual contact. Abundant for many years, they had increased rapidly with the increasing food potential from the human population, which waxed more wasteful with increasing wealth. The landfill site by the approach road was a particularly handy bonus.

It became illegal in 1987 to take wild birds' eggs and from three years after that until 1930 Walney supported a flourishing tern colony. The ternery suffered more severely from gull harassment, largely the theft of eggs and chicks, as the larger birds waxed more numerous. Eventually the victims abandoned the site, along with the smaller

100. *Common Terns*

black-headed gulls, and set up new quarters on Foulney Island. In 1967 some elected to return to Walney, but their stay lasted only four years before they left again - along with the smaller gulls.

Much research has been carried out here on the gulls by ornithologists from the Animal Behaviour Department of the University of Oxford under the tutelage of the famous and inimitable Professor Niko Tinbergen. He shared a Nobel Prize with his own eccentric and delightful tutor, Konrad Lorenz, who is usually depicted as a "Mother Goose" leading his family of 'imprinted' goslings over land or through water.

Tinbergen's most notable work relevant to the Walney studies was the well known "The Herring Gulls' World", Collins, 1953. This followed "The Study of Instinct", 1951, which was greeted as "The classical text - a milestone in the development of ethology" (the study of behaviour). Data appearing in these texts concerned the gulls' displays, feeding behaviour, nest density and egg colour.

We observed considerable variety in their eggs, which included every variant from those pigmented with a rich khaki brown, heavily blotched with black to those with fainter markings on a pale bluish green ground. One nest with two eggs had the two extremes lying side by side, the paler one only faintly figured and resembling a duck's egg. This is unusual from the same mother. Had someone been meddling to see if the parent birds noticed?

As so often, their feeding sites were littered with expectorated food remains. Crop pellets were, round, oval or tapering to a point. Some were composed solely of chaff, probably scavenged from fodder put out for cattle or sheep. Others were of macerated crab shells or pulverised shell-fish plus a motley of unidentifiable items from the trash dump. Those having the consistency of dried dung sometimes contained viable seeds, a source of newcomers, often arable weeds, to the plant community. The content of those having the consistency of desiccated porridge remained unidentified,

Mostly the nests were on dunes or sandy grassland but some of those on the pebble beaches were only a few yards from the sea and surely extremely vulnerable to inundation by quite minor waves. Water was currently lapping at the basal layers of egg wrack which formed the foundation of one nest below a variety of bric-a-brac from the driftline and more traditional plant material.

101. Eider Drake

The eider ducks, which first bred here in 1941, built more substantial and comfortable structures among longish grass, a cosy eider-down of contour feathers plucked from the duck's breast pushed up all around their portly figures. Unlike the gulls, they tolerated a close approach, as is usual in their more familiar terrain of Scottish heather. They rely on their near perfect camouflage and stillness to save them from predators. If a nest had to be left the eggs would be covered with down. One sitting duck which I photographed had chosen a spot only two or three yards from an occupied gull's nest. Which, I wondered, was there first?

The eider drakes were fraternising in matey gatherings along the shoreline, permanently off duty, at least until the family hatched. Some wrapped their webbed feet over dry pebbles, others rode the gentle swell. Only the triangular heads of these blatantly black and white show-offs, with their evocative crooning calls, showed their relationship to their conscientious spouses.

By the 1970s the eider population had built up to around two hundred pairs, this possibly, it is conjectured, because the ducklings are herded out onto the sea soon after hatching. With much larger families than the terns and by linking up with others, there are enough Mums around, not feeding, to protect them from the depredations of the gulls - rather like penguin chicks in their chilly creches where they gang up against preda-tory great skuas.

Eiders are northern birds, most at home in Norway and Iceland and breeding scarcely any further south than Walney in Great Britain and Ireland, although they may venture south in winter. They are sea duck, diving for food on the ocean bed and with a particular liking for sea mussels.

The shelduck and mallard which had formerly nested in good numbers on Walney were not so fortunate and had dwindled seriously due to predation of their young. This danger is also very real on Cardiff's home island of Flatholm, where only remnants of the big families of shelducks succeed in making the three mile swim from the island cliffs to the mud flats of the estuarine shore which they must reach to find their traditional food of minute sea snails. Wise shelduck mothers take their broods to sea at night to escape the swooping gulls. No duck, however dedicated, can protect twelve or thirteen bobbing ducklings from the marauders.

Fully grown ducks flying into the reserve in winter are not bothered by the gulls. Teal and wigeon build up sometimes to a thousand birds, with around half as many eiders and shelducks and more modest numbers of mallard, pochard, scaup, pintail, long-tailed duck and those elegant maritime fishing ducks, the red-breasted mergansers. Scoters, the most dedicated sea duck, usually remain well offshore.

Both oyster catchers and ringed plovers were nesting on the beaches. The first can build up to flocks of twenty thousand in winter - or sixty thousand prior to the freezing winter of 1962-63, but with an average of around fifteen thousand. Knot, too, can number fifteen thousand during

102. Red-breasted Mergansers

those cold, short days, dunlin six thousand, redshank four thousand and curlew a thousand.

These are the ornithological highlights. The smaller passage migrants that keep bird ringers so busy on more remote sea bird islands are not attracted to the bedlam of the gullery in any numbers, with so much welcoming mainland coast at their disposal round about.

Passing migrants will usually be following the coast, flying high and likely to plump down anywhere to rest and feed. The more usual island bird reserve offers a welcome haven in an unwelcoming expanse of ocean and then often only a small amount of precious cover in a semi desert of windswept turf. This is the cover in which the ornithologists site their bird traps to send them on their way as numbered emissaries contributing to our knowledge of migration and much more if they can be recovered.

It is thought that some small birds following the coast prefer the two short sea trips to and from the Isle of Man when commuting to Scotland, rather than following the insinuations of the coast around the various firths and inlets.

Resident passerines are almost limited to meadow pipits and skylarks. They nested among heather and bracken but have had diminishing success in the expanding gull citadel.

Some of the over wintering wildfowl are attracted to the very different habitat of the saltmarsh. Here they can feed on mudflats at low water and retreat to the grassy saltings at high. There is no cover there, but comfortingly uninterrupted views all around so that any predatoror can be spotted while still a long way off.

Two saltings habitats are sharply demarcated by a vertical erosion cliff, where the sea is eating into land built up in earlier times. These earth clifflets can be two to three feet high, following sinuous creeks and drainage gullies and exposing successive horizons of soil, sometimes with narrow layers of drifted shells interposed. Successive layers are not much more than a centimetre deep, as though deposited by individual high tides. As the gullies broaden the land between becomes islanded and worn down to cylindrical, turf-topped islets.

These saltings nourish excellent lamb and sheep keep the salt marsh grass and red fescue nibbled off short. The roots are more spreading than the above ground parts and help to delay disintegration of the isolated tumps. All the soil removed is being transported elsewhere. It would be interesting to know where it finishes up.

An unusual component of the marsh community is the lax-flowered sea lavender (*Limonium humile*), with leaves scattered along the angular branches and narrower than those of the common species, with which it may hybridise. This is commoner on the Irish coast than the British.

103. Lax flowered Sea Lavender

In places currents were benign enough to allow the displaced soil to remain stable sufficiently long for a grass sward to build up at the lower level, this preceded by glasswort (Salicornia) and other saltmarsh pioneers. Most of these are succulent and resistant to both real and physiological drought, but are annuals and can be swept away in winter turbulence before the binding grass has a chance to establish. Sea smoothed, multi coloured pebbles roll around on these vulnerable surfaces when stirred at high tide, having an abrasive effect.

On level strands elsewhere pebbles may get thrown landward to build up elevated storm beaches. Static pebbles along the crest and inland facing slopes get colonised by crustose lichens, which need light to grow, like other plants. Storm waves can roll the pebbles over, casting the lichens into darkness where they die, adding their tiny quota of organic matter to trapped seaweed and other debris, to form the beginning of a soil, while more lichens start the process again on the upturned surfaces. Wind-borne seeds germinate in moisture trapped between the pebbles and the succession builds up - patchily, depending on subsequent slides and jostlings.

Most colourful of the large storm beach plants flowering in late spring were the yellow horned poppies, with their long, stem-like pods. Another was viper's bugloss, the pink buds turning blue as the flowers opened. Also in this family is hound's tongue, with its clusters of wine-red flowers and quartet of nutlets beset with bristles for ease of transport.

104. Oyster Plant

Most exciting for botanists hailing from the South was the oyster plant (*Mertensia maritima*), also known as northern shorewort. This is another of the more ebullient members of the forget-me-not family, along with the bugloss and hound's tongue. It, too, has blue flowers which are pink at first but more bell-shaped. The whole plant is smooth and hairless, whereas the others are beset with bristly hairs.

Leaves are fleshy and are said to taste of oysters, while the whole, mat forming plant is blue-grey in colour. Essentially northern, from North Lancashire and Northumberland to Shetland, the species has, or had, a few outliers in Norfolk and North Wales, but has been decreasing everywhere for over half a century. It grows normally on shingle beaches. Most at home from Jutland to Iceland, it may well become one of our rarities lost to global warming.

Another pebble plant of special interest is the poisonous henbane, with its weird pale yellow flowers veined with purple. The fruiting stems uncoil to bear long lines of capsules packed with tiny brown seeds beloved by the smaller finches. This is boosted by gull guano and is a feature of gull colonies on Puffin Island off Anglesey and Steepholm Island off North Somerset. It also gets a boost around populous rabbit warrens on the chalk downs of Southern England - and there was no shortage of rabbits at Walney.

All these except the oyster plant are coarse, upstanding species, unpalatable to livestock and with roots penetrating deeply among the pebbles in search of the elusive water - some of which condenses as internal dew at night. Another was the showy and even taller corn sow thistle, which is more characteristic of pebbly wasteland than cornfields in these days of lavish herbicide application. Patches of this beautified shingle heaps ponding back water in the various wetland habitats. Celery-leaved buttercups and marsh bedstraw featured in the ponds, with marginal sedges, rushes and marsh pennywort swards.

An animal of note here is the natterjack toad (*Bufo calamita*), also to be found on nearby sands in coastal Lancashire. Nationally it is vey rare, almost confined to sandy coasts and more inland heaths in Surrey and Dorset. This latter site is blessed also with populations of the rare smooth snake and sand lizard. An isolated and threatened population of larger, darker natterjack toads occurs in County Kerry in South-west Ireland.

Flowers were few among the tufts of marram and soldierly lines of sand sedge on the dunes and consisted mostly of wasteland weeds of the dandelion, cress and chickweed fraternities, also black nightshade, a relative of henbane in the sometimes so palatable and yet potentially poisonous family of the Solanaceae. Most attractive were the little wild pansies or heartsease.

105. Natterjack Toad

LIST OF ILLUSTRATIONS

54. Early colonisation by Thrift
55. Mountain Everlasting or Cat's Foot
56. Scottish Lovage
57. Purple Milk Vetch and Pyramidal Bugle
58. Sea Arrow Grass and Least Soft Brome Grass
59. Irish Eyebright, Thyme Broomrape and Thyme
60. Herons at Nest
61. Beaked Tasselweed and Enteromorpha
62. Donkeys and ponies on the Sandflats
63. Yellow Wort and Yellow Rattle
64. Prickly Saltwort and Frosted Orache
65. Cranefly, Rose Chafer Beetle and Rose Pea Gall
66. Fairy Ring Fungus, St. George's Mushroom and Puffball
67. Scytosiphon, Halidrys and Nitophyllum seaweeds
68. Sea Spurge, Sand Couch and Sea Couch
69. Lining up for Curragh Race
70. Ringed Plover and Sandwich Tern
71. Sea Slater and Dwarf Sea Plantain
72. Cory's and Manx Shearwaters at Sea
73. "Cromlech" Picnic Table

74. Aran Bee and Bulbous Buttercup
75. Transparent and Six Spot Burnet Moths
76. Dascillus Beetle and Garden Chafer
77. O'Brien's Castle
78. Babington's Leek
79. Pipewort, Perfoliate Pondweed and Nuttall's Waterweed
80. Deer Grass, Black Bog Rush and Viviparous Fescue
81. Spotted Rock Rose and Yellow Bartsia
82. St. Dabeoc's Heath and Mackay's Heath
83. Narrow-leaved Bog Cotton and Bog Asphodel
84. Barnacle Geese
85. White-tailed Eagle, for which Achill Island is named
86. Mussel Rafts
87. Black Crowberry and Heath Milkwort
88. Heath Rush and Mat Grass with discarded tufts
89. New Zealand Cabbage Tree
90. Wood Pigeons
91. Great Tits
92. Bilberry or Whortleberry
93. Pink Purslane
94. Loghtan Sheep
95. Hooded Crow